CONTEMPLATION AND COMPASSION

TRADITIONS OF CHRISTIAN SPIRITUALITY SERIES

At the Fountain of Elijah: The Carmelite Tradition
Wilfrid McGreal O. Carm.

*Eyes to See, Ears to Hear: An Introduction to Ignatian
Spirituality*
David Lonsdale

*God's Lovers in an Age of Anxiety: The Medieval English
Mystics*
Joan M. Nuth

Journeys on the Edges: The Celtic Tradition
Thomas O'Loughlin

Mysticism and Prophecy: The Dominican Tradition
Richard Woods OP

Our Restless Heart: The Augustinian Tradition
Thomas F. Martin OSA

The Poetic Imagination: An Anglican Spiritual Tradition
William Countryman

Poverty and Joy: The Franciscan Tradition
William J. Short OFM

Prayer and Community: The Benedictine Tradition
Columba Stewart OSB

The Spirit of Worship: The Liturgical Tradition
Susan J. White

Standing in God's Holy Fire: The Byzantine Tradition
John Anthony McGuckin

The Way of Simplicity: The Cistercian Tradition
Esther de Waal

CONTEMPLATION AND COMPASSION

The Victorine Tradition

STEVEN CHASE

SERIES EDITOR:
Philip Sheldrake

ORBIS BOOKS
Maryknoll, New York 10545

Founded in 1970, Orbis Books endeavors to publish works that enlighten the mind, nourish the spirit, and challenge the conscience. The publishing arm of the Maryknoll Fathers & Brothers, Orbis seeks to explore the global dimensions of the Christian faith and mission, to invite dialogue with diverse cultures and religious traditions, and to serve the cause of reconciliation and peace. The books published reflect the views of their authors and do not represent the official position of the Society. To learn more about Maryknoll and Orbis Books, please visit our website at www.maryknoll.org.

First published in Great Britain in 2003 by
Darton, Longman and Todd Ltd
1 Spencer Court
140–142 Wandsworth High Street
London SW18 4JJ
Great Britain

First published in the USA in 2003 by
Orbis Books
P.O. Box 308
Maryknoll, New York 10545–0308
U.S.A.

Orbis ISBN 1–57075–473–X

The Scripture quotations in this publication are taken from the New Revised Standard Version © 1989, 1995. Division of Christian Education of the National Council of the Churches of Christ in the United States of America.

Printed and bound in Great Britain.

Library of Congress Cataloging-in-Publication Data

Chase, Steven.
    Contemplation and compassion : the Victorine tradition / by Steven Chase.
        p.   cm.—(Traditions of Christian spirituality series)
    ISBN 1–57075–473–X (pbk.)
    1. Saint-Victor (Abbey : Paris, France) 2. Spirituality—History—Middle Ages, 600–1500. 3. Augustinian Canons—France—Paris—Spiritual life. I. Title. II. Traditions of Christian spirituality.
BX2615.P35   C48   2003
248′.0944′361—dc21   2002013706

In memory of

Reverend David Miles (1962 - 2001)

Now there are two things that restore
divine likeness in humanity:
contemplation of truth and the practice of virtue.

Hugh of St Victor, *Didascalicon*, I. viii

CONTENTS

Preface by Philip Sheldrake   9

Prologue   13

Introduction: A Century of Spiritual Awakening   15

1. Victorine Masters: Patterns of Integration   26

2. Mapping the Spiritual Journey   43

3. Exegesis: Literal, Spiritual, Visual   63

4. The Paths of Knowledge and Love   83

5. Mystical Theology: The Mystery of the Real   103

6. Contemplation as a Way of Life   127

Conclusion: Implications for Contemporary Spirituality   148

Notes   155

Bibliography   167

PREFACE TO THE SERIES

Nowadays, in the western world, there is a widespread hunger for spirituality in all its forms. This is not confined to traditional religious people let alone to regular churchgoers. The desire for resources to sustain the spiritual quest has led many people to seek wisdom in unfamiliar places. Some have turned to cultures other than their own. The fascination with Native American or Aboriginal Australian spiritualities is a case in point. Other people have been attracted by the religions of India and Tibet or the Jewish Kabbalah and Sufi mysticism. One problem is that, in comparison to other religions, Christianity is not always associated in people's minds with 'spirituality'. The exceptions are a few figures from the past who have achieved almost cult status such as Hildegard of Bingen or Meister Eckhart. This is a great pity, for Christianity East and West over two thousand years has given birth to an immense range of spiritual wisdom. Many traditions continue to be active today. Others that were forgotten are being rediscovered and reinterpreted.

It is a long time since an extended series of introductions to Christian spiritual traditions has been available in English. Given the present climate, it is an opportune moment for a new series which will help more people to be aware of the great spiritual riches available within the Christian tradition.

The overall purpose of the series is to make selected spiritual traditions available to a contemporary readership. The books seek to provide accurate and balanced historical and thematic treatments of their subjects. The authors are also conscious of the need to make connections with contemporary experience and values without being artificial or reducing a tradition to one dimension. The authors are well versed in reliable scholarship about the traditions they describe. However, their intention is that the books should be fresh in style and accessible to the general reader.

One problem that such a series inevitably faces is the word 'spirituality'. For example, it is increasingly used beyond religious circles and does not necessarily imply a faith tradition. Again, it could mean substantially different things for a Christian and a Buddhist. Within Christianity itself, the word in its modern sense is relatively recent. The reality that it stands for differs subtly in the different contexts of time and place. Historically, 'spirituality' covers a breadth of human experience and a wide range of values and practices.

No single definition of 'spirituality' has been imposed on the authors in this series. Yet, despite the breadth of the series there is a sense of a common core in the writers themselves and in the traditions they describe. All Christian spiritual traditions have their source in three things. First, while drawing on ordinary experience and even religious insights from elsewhere, Christian spiritualities are rooted in the Scriptures and particularly in the Gospels. Second, spiritual traditions are not derived from abstract theory but from attempts to live out gospel values in a positive yet critical way within specific historical and cultural contexts. Third, the experiences and insights of individuals and groups are not isolated but are related to the wider Christian tradition of beliefs, practices and community life. From a Christian perspective, spirituality is not just concerned with prayer or even with narrowly religious activities. It concerns the whole of human life, viewed in terms of a conscious relationship with God, in Jesus Christ, through the indwelling of the Holy Spirit and within a community of believers.

The series as a whole includes traditions that probably would not have appeared twenty years ago. The authors themselves have been encouraged to challenge, where appropriate, inaccurate assumptions about their particular tradition. While conscious of their own biases, authors have none the less sought to correct the imbalances of the past. Previous understandings of what is mainstream or 'orthodox' sometimes need to be questioned. People or practices that became marginal demand to be re-examined. Studies of spirituality in the past frequently underestimated or ignored the role of women. Sometimes the treatments of spiritual traditions were culturally one-sided because they were written from an uncritical Western European or North Atlantic perspective.

However, any series is necessarily selective. It cannot hope to do full justice to the extraordinary variety of Christian spiritual traditions. The principles of selection are inevitably open to question. I hope that an appropriate balance has been maintained between a sense of the likely readership on the one hand and the dangers of narrowness on the other. In the end, choices had to be made and the result is inevitably weighted in favour of traditions that have achieved 'classic' status or which seem to capture the contemporary imagination. Within these limits, I trust that the series will offer a reasonably balanced account of what the Christian spiritual tradition has to offer.

As editor of the series I would like to thank all the authors who agreed to contribute and for the stimulating conversations and correspondence that sometimes resulted. I am especially grateful for the high quality of their work which made my task so much easier. Editing such a series is a complex undertaking. I have worked closely throughout with the editorial team of Darton, Longman and Todd and Robert Ellsberg of Orbis Books. I am immensely grateful to them for their friendly support and judicious advice. Without them this series would never have come together.

PHILIP SHELDRAKE
Sarum College, Salisbury

PROLOGUE

In Victorine spirituality contemplation gives birth to charity. Charity involves love, service to others, social justice, liberation, healing, and compassion. The Victorines insist that the final goal of the life of faith is not the contemplative enjoyment of God in itself, 'but consists in taking on Christ, and therefore returning from ecstasy to loving service of neighbor.'[1]

We can look at the parts of Victorine spirituality metaphorically as a set of mirrors. Each mirror reflects back upon the whole: contemplation, compassion and charity. The Victorine mirror of, for instance, scholarly and meditative study of the Bible reflects the visions held within the mirrors of creative theological inquiry, the spiritual journey, liturgical regularity, pastoral authority, and profoundly innovative contemplative teaching and practice. We also see in Victorine teaching that contemplation and prayer are reflected in the mirror of theology. Theology in turn sees itself in the mirror of biblical interpretation, which itself reflects the gaze of symbolic and sacramental cosmology. Symbols are reflected in the mirrors of liturgy, anagogical ascent to God, and participation in the presence of God. The mirror of tradition reflects the mirror of experience. Experience returns a gaze of deep wonder into that same mirror of tradition. The mirror that is empty reflects the mirror that is full. The deep mystery of God is mirrored in simple acts of kindness and gratitude. The book of nature reflects the book of the soul; love reflects knowledge, knowledge reflects love; wisdom and virtue see the face of one in the face of the other. And all, like a many-faceted gem, reflect the grace of compassionate charity.

Today this is somewhat difficult to grasp. We are mostly comfortable with our distinctions. We practise self-contained disciplines. We are satisfied with our own, unique ways of seeing God. We are quite good at itemizing and separating; we are not so good at unifying.

The Victorines would have found our modern separations incomprehensible. This does not mean that they were not capable of fine distinctions. They certainly *do* write theology, they *do* interpret Scripture, they *do* participate in liturgy, they *do* practise contemplation. But these separate elements of their spirituality are all undertaken only with the understanding that each element is integral to the whole and that the whole is greater than the sum of its parts. This 'greater whole' consists in taking on Christ; it is love, charity, compassion. In what follows we will find that various mirrors of Victorine spirituality are capable, when focused on a single point, of igniting a holocaust of charity.

This book will be divided into thematic chapters that represent some of the primary *elements* of Victorine spirituality. But it is the Victorine ideal of *integration in the name of compassionate charity* that will prove to be the most useful and valuable for contemporary Christian spirituality.

INTRODUCTION:
A CENTURY OF SPIRITUAL AWAKENING

VICTORINE SPIRITUALITY IN PERSPECTIVE

A Collect for purity from the *Book of Common Prayer* brings us before God with the following words:

> Almighty God,
> unto whom all hearts are open,
> all desires known,
> and from whom no secrets are hid:
> cleanse the thoughts of our hearts
> by the inspiration of thy Holy Spirit,
> that we may perfectly love thee,
> and worthily magnify thy holy name;
> through Christ our Lord. Amen.
> (*Book of Common Prayer*, p. 323)

Few words in such a short space could better encapsulate the Victorine spiritual tradition. The spiritual journey is outlined in the words of petition that move from purification to illumination to perfection. Hearts rest open in contemplation before God. The phrase 'thoughts of our hearts' echoes the intimate relation between knowledge and love. There is a hint of apophatic or negative theology in the words 'secret' and 'hid', yet also of cataphatic or positive theology in the confession that 'all hearts are open . . . no secrets are hid'. There is a longing to participate with God in the very breath or 'inspiration' of God. Mystery and holiness are the habitation of God, are God's true names. Love is the perfection of our very being. An invocation to the Trinity – Almighty God, Christ our Lord, and

Holy Spirit – serves as a structural doctrine of the Collect. And finally, the prayer reflects an intensely personal relation with God, even as the simple word 'our' confesses to community and shared adoration. In these few words we do indeed, as we will see in the following chapters of this book, find a vivid summary of the depth and wisdom of Victorine spirituality.

The Victorine spiritual tradition, originating at the Abbey of St Victor in Paris, was one of the most creative, exciting, and productive traditions of the Middle Ages. It was a primary source of the great spiritual awakening of the twelfth century, representing an evocative transitional phase that brought the monastic mystical tradition into contact with practices of intellectual reflection emerging in the schools of Paris. The Victorines as an order of Canons Regular spanned the centuries from the dynamic spiritual flowering of the twelfth century down to the French Revolution when the community was finally suppressed. They played a central role in making the mystical theology of Pseudo-Dionysius influential in the West. The Victorines brought together scholarship, mysticism, liturgy, exegesis, aesthetics, ethics, contemplation, and compassion into a fruitful and comprehensive synthesis – a synthesis that is capable of providing profound insights and direction for contemporary prayer formation. Contemplation itself was, for the Victorines, not simply a discipline or technique for prayer; it was a way of life.

To retrieve the wisdom of the Victorine spiritual tradition is to offer to contemporary men and women access to a way of being with God steeped in Scripture, theology, liturgy, prayer, and service. The Victorines were as comfortable with their commitment to acknowledge the presence of God in and through all things as they were with the idea of an unfathomable God of mystery whose primary attribute often seems to be complete absence. Their use of symbols and allegory in contemplation and biblical interpretation stretches our imagination and reasoning capacities. At the same time their exploration of negative (apophatic) and positive (cataphatic) forms of theology lead ever deeper into the loving heart of

God. Victorine mystical theology also provides models for our contemporary recovery of the essential nature of dialogue between theology and spirituality.

THE TWELFTH CENTURY: A CENTURY OF SPIRITUAL AWAKENING

Few if any periods in Western spirituality have seen such a rise in concentration of spiritual masters or writers on contemplation as did the twelfth century. In this, the Victorines were not alone. Bernard of Clairvaux, William of St Thierry, Hildegard of Bingen, Aelred of Rievaux, Joachim of Fiore, and Elizabeth of Schönau, and others, were also recasting Western Christendom's vision of spirituality, prayer, and contemplation. The twelfth century was, in every sense, a century of spiritual awakening, integrating and incorporating the riches of the past. As Grover Zinn has said of the Victorines in particular:

> In the Western Church it remained for the 12th century mystical writers to gather up a wealth of inherited material, combine it with their own experiences and observations, and begin a systematic literary presentation of the ascetic life and a careful analysis of contemplative experiences. As scholars have pointed out in recent years, the 12th century was a decisive turning point in the history of spirituality [during which time] the distinctive elements of almost all later medieval spirituality and piety were formulated.[1]

Scholars have noted that the decisive turning point in Western Christian spirituality between the years 1050 and 1215 effected as deep a transformation as the fragmentation of the Church in the sixteenth century or even as the spread of Christianity in the first three centuries after Christ. During this period a renewed search for the 'apostolic life' resulted in a large number of new or reformed groups including Cistercians, Carthusians, Premonstratensians, Waldensians, Franciscans, and Dominicans as well as Victorines. Characteristic to all of these orders and groups, to one degree or another, was a new sense of compassionate service to others. This was expressed most often through charitable acts, preaching, and a new sense of duty to love and worship God through poverty, through private prayer, and spiritual growth. This urgent sense of reform and renewal signalled the early pre-stages of the mendicant movement and the growth of lay piety, both of which would later influence Christian commitment to poverty, the imitation of Christ, and the 'apostolic way'.

The century also witnessed the slow movement from an oral tradition to written secular and ecclesiastical laws and to written forms of pedagogy. It was a period of papal reform and of crusades to the Holy Land. The century saw a general movement from monastic and cathedral schools to the early stages of the rise of the great universities at Paris, Oxford, and Bologna which were to become centres of theology, philosophy, and science in the thirteenth century. It was a century of 'courtly love' which was adapted to mystical experience and writing that resulted in a systematic ordering of love, charity and knowledge.

The first steps in a new devotion to the humanity of Christ began in this century and flowered in the thirteenth century that followed. Perhaps most basic and influential of all, Christians of the twelfth century participated in a growing sense of the inter-connectedness and holiness of all things – what we might call a 'sacramental cosmology'. This participation was based in no small part on the creative use of symbols and the symbolic imagination as well as the use of reason and the will to encounter and communicate the sacred nature of all good things of God's creation.

The twelfth century, unfortunately, also had its dark side. The Crusades resulted in the death and displacement of thousands of people. The Church issued anti-Jewish polemic which resulted in popular violence against Jews and discriminatory legislation in the Third and Fourth Lateran Councils (1179 and 1215). Popular movements beginning in this century such as the Waldensians and Cathari (known later as the Albigensians in Southern France) were seen as institutionally and theologically threatening to the Church. Though formal inquisitions against these groups did not commence until the thirteenth century, twelfth-century legislation such as the decree of Gratian (1140), the resolutions of the Third Lateran Council, and decrees by both kings and popes branded these groups as heretical and spoke of their 'crimes' in terms of high treason.

Given this creative energy and experimentation, scholars of the last seventy years have consistently approached the twelfth century as a period of fundamental change.[2] Writers have noted in turn that the twelfth century ushered in a new period of humanism, that it was a golden age of renaissance, and that it was a century of new discoveries in the areas of psychology, nature, and the arts. The period is said to have initiated and used scientific method. And for over thirty years writers have spoken of the twelfth-century 'discovery of the individual'. The writers, teachers, and spiritual practitioners of the period returned again and again to issues focused on the individual quest, personal experience, and self-expression.

Without denying any of these aspects of the twelfth century, Caroline Walker Bynum has recently cautioned that a more nuanced assessment of the core initiatives of the twelfth century must include not only (1) the 'discovery of the self', but also (2) the place of the self in the context of community. By this she does not mean to deny the emphasis on the individual, but rather to point out the equally important twelfth-century trait of 'belonging'.

The twelfth-century 'individual' acquired a sense of belonging within a group by adopting a model that simultaneously shaped both the 'outer person' (behaviour in a group) and the 'inner person' (the soul). For the Victorines there were a range of such 'models' from the past that served to shape spirituality and to form the 'inner and outer person'. Among the 'models' consciously employed by the Victorines were those of the primitive Church, the apostolic life, the saints, the desert and Patristic fathers and mothers, stories and symbols from

Scripture, the anagogic or 'uplifting' symbols and rites of the liturgy, the accumulated Christian wisdom in meditation and contemplation, and, of course, Christ himself. The variety of these 'models' prompted an increase in the number and variety of twelfth-century religious communities. Some failed, others flourished. But common to them all was the spiritual growth that flourished in the context of the relation between self and community. In sum, during the twelfth century, personal spiritual growth flowered in the context of community.

The Victorines grew, contributed to, and prospered in this new twelfth-century environment. The century is not (as is sometimes pictured) the beginning of a march toward more and more private and individualistic piety that would increasingly bypass ecclesiastical structures. Rather, the turn inward was simultaneously a turn toward relationship, toward community, toward friendship, and toward love and compassion. This new discovery of the spirituality of the self within community was itself treated as a step toward God. The Victorines, perhaps more than any other group whose roots took hold in the soil of this awakening century, lived, modelled, and wrote explicitly about this growing consciousness of the intimate connections among self, community, and God.

Though the Victorines inhabited a particular place and time, there is what we might call a 'universalism' to the particular Victorine charism. Victorines in community directed their example, teaching, and words toward concrete experience. In doing so they provided penetrating analysis of spiritual wisdom directed at concrete spiritual practice. The Victorines explored what today we might call the psychological dimensions of experience. But this exploration was far from a simplistic reduction of all human experience to psychological states. Victorines plotted the widest possible range of human experience. Their insights into the nature of the self mined human attributes including sensual perception, the intuitive imagination, the operations of the mind, heart, body and soul, discernment of spiritual consolations and desolations, practices of contemplation, the characteristic of wonder, and the intuition of divine mystery.

THE ABBEY OF ST VICTOR AT PARIS

Favoured by the highest officials of Church and state, a haven for scholars and training school for many bishops, the Abbey of St Victor at Paris was justly revered.[3] William of Champeaux, whom his most distinguished pupil, Abelard, admitted to be 'the first dialectician of his age' founded the abbey. After a celebrated conflict between William and Abelard over the subject of 'universals', William retired from his position as master in the schools of Paris in 1108. In that year he set up a small community at an old hermitage on the Seine just outside the gates of Paris. Evidently with no intention of founding a new order, William wanted to retire to a life of prayer and monkish study. But, based in part on William's fame, a community grew around him. With its growth the community added a contemplative element, a new sense of liturgical formation, and a love of learning and scholarship foreign to most other communities of Augustinian Canons. William left St Victor's to become Bishop of Châlons in 1113.

Upon William's departure, his disciple, Gilduin, was elected as the first abbot. Gilduin was in many ways responsible for the early fame of St Victor's. He was a leader capable of drawing and motivating strong personalities and intellects, of organizing and administering the abbey, and of gaining the necessary external support to establish the new community of Regular Canons under the *Rule of St Augustine*. Under Gilduin, St Victor's became the head of an order with its own general chapters. His tutelage ensured that the abbey would maintain a vigorous spiritual and intellectual life, and remain open to new theological developments in the schools of Paris that other monastics tended to shun. Though papal action was required in 1172 to remove an incompetent abbot, the abbey at St Victor flourished throughout the twelfth and thirteenth centuries. The abbey, with its magnificent library, survived until the French revolution.

MONKS AND CANONS

The twelfth century was, as we have seen, a century of evangelical awakening. Both clergy and laity were stirred by the idea of religious renewal and a return to the primitive Church of the 'pure' gospel that arose from that pristine time. They were stirred to the perfection and dignity of the apostolic life or the *vita apostolica*, which was equated with following Christ, poverty, personal sanctity or holiness, and preaching repentance.

The two great expressions of this passionate return to the apostolic life were the Cistercians and the Augustinian Canons, also known as Regular Canons or Austin Canons. The abbey at St Victor in Paris was, as we have seen, a community of Augustinian Canons. Though the Cistercians and Augustinian Canons as twelfth-century expressions of apostolic fervour were similar in many ways, many scholars have pointed out their essentially different, even antithetical ways of living the apostolic life.

The Cistercians were monks seeking to reform the older Benedictine order. Founded in 1098 at Cîteaux, Cistercians intended from the beginning to cultivate a strenuous life of prayer (usually *lectio divina*), liturgical worship (referred to as the *Opus Dei* or work of God) and labour. Though the *Rule of St Benedict* was common to both Cistercians ('White Monks') and Benedictines ('Black Monks'), the Cistercians were committed from the beginning to an austere life which they felt was more in keeping with both Benedict's *Rule* and the gospel.[4]

The Augustinian Canons were not monks. The status of canons was something new in the medieval life. They were not, strictly speaking, a monastic order. 'Canons' can be defined most simply as collegiate clergy.[5] They were ordained clergy who wished to live a common life of poverty, celibacy, and obedience to a superior without withdrawal from the world.

By the thirteenth century there were thousands of such communities, though many were quite small. And though they were originally active in preaching and teaching, as well as in establishing hospitals and refuges for the sick and poor, many of the larger houses later became virtually indistinguishable from older monastic orders.

But throughout the twelfth century the essential differences remained. Caroline Walker Bynum has shown that perhaps the essential difference was the Augustinian's commitment to spiritual edification through both word (writing, teaching and preaching) and through the personal example of a virtuous life lived according to the will of God through identification with Christ. For the Augustinian Canons of the twelfth century, moral education through word and deed, through speech and conduct, would become the most natural path of spiritual formation and growth.

RULE OF ST AUGUSTINE: A GUIDE TO THE SPIRITUAL LIFE

The abbey at St Victor reflects the general evolution of the Augustinian Canons in the twelfth century. As we have seen, for the Victorines, turning inward in exploration of self and soul went hand in hand with a sense of belonging to a group. The group that formed outside of Paris at St Victor was guided and inspired by the *Rule* of the great fifth-century bishop, St Augustine of Hippo. Monastic rules were intended as guidelines for living within a community centred in all things on God. As one might imagine, rules were as various as the times, places, individuals, and communities that formed them. Today as well, men and women of faith develop rules for living, whether in community or in private devotion to focus their attention on God.

There is a long history of controversy and debate concerning the authenticity of *The Rule of St Augustine*. But whatever its origin, the *Rule* has, over the centuries, proven to be flexible and adaptable to a variety of communities in a wide range of times and locations. Though the authorship has been called into question, there is a real sense of spiritual continuity between Augustine's influence on his own community at Hippo and the twelfth-century communities of the Regular Canons that took up and modified the precepts of the *Rule*. The *Rule* is grounded in evangelical values and impulses based in part on Acts 4:32 which states that, 'the whole group of those who believed were of one heart and soul'. As a key charism and value, the *Rule* thus states that 'The main purpose for your having come together is to live harmoniously in your house, intent upon God in oneness of mind and heart' (I.1).[6] This is an excellent summary of the Victorine ideal: the spiritual and contemplative exploration of the inner person accomplished under the guidance, supervision, and love of the community intent on union with God through imitation of Christ in order to become an example for others. The imitation of Christ showed itself in how one lived, both within community and in compassionate charity toward others; it showed itself, in a word, in one's 'behaviour'. The twelfth century rediscovered the concept of *gestus* ('behaviour' in gesture, bearing, and humility) as an important aspect of teaching by example. Hugh of St Victor, in fact, writing for novices, wrote a unique treatise on the meanings attached to details of exemplary behaviour.[7] Such behaviour was intended to both reflect and teach the apostolic life.

Augustine's *Rule* is an early and successful attempt to regulate monastic life. Its influence is obvious in many other monastic Rules. In addition to the Canon movement of the eleventh and twelfth centuries of which the Victorines were a part, it was utilized in the mendicant movement of Franciscan and Dominican friars of the twelfth and thirteenth centuries. Today the *Rule of St Augustine* guides the religious life of the Order of St Augustine organized in its present form in 1256. Although monasticism is popularly associated with Cassian in Egypt and the Desert Fathers, the African monks inspired by St Augustine's *Rule* became foundation stones of Western monasticism long before the time of St Benedict and his *Rule*.

Augustine's *Rule* fostered ascetical ideals, humanism, mysticism, the apostolic life, scholarly study, contemplation, and imitation of the life of Christ. Speaking of the *Rule* Mary T. Clark writes:

> To follow the *Rule of St. Augustine* is to make a spiritual ascent to that Beauty which is God, the Splendor of Truth. Generosity is the response to this Beauty, which is reflected, in a true community of one heart and one mind, in the one Christ after the model of the first Christians at Jerusalem. A fervent [community under the Rule] is a microcosm of the City of God.[8]

Such was the charitable intent of the Victorine contemplative community in twelfth-century Paris: generosity of personal response to the beauty and truth of God charitably regulated within in the context of supportive community.

1. VICTORINE MASTERS: PATTERNS OF INTEGRATION

THE TAPESTRY OF VICTORINE MASTERS

As any gardener knows, to find balance between the lush profusion of nature and the aesthetical requirements of garden harmony is a search that never ends. Yet the gardener seeks to find some kind of structuring unity in the lavish bio-diversity of creation. Design is built into chaos through tricks of colour, shape, texture, height, border, background, fragrance, blooming time, pathways, pools, statuary, varying shrub and ornamental tree, annual and perennial. One creative garden designer has recently suggested a pattern that creates order in her garden by dividing it into a series of randomly shaped patchwork blocks. She calls her design a 'quilt garden', and it is obvious that she truly delights in achieving harmony and unity through diversity:

> Adjoining blocks in my crazy quilt of a garden are gener-
> ally coordinated by a color theme. The front yard is
> planned around the color yellow, the side yard orange,
> and the backyard wine-red . . . Within the dominate color
> scheme for each area a great deal of experimentation is
> possible . . . And as a quilter might finish things off with an
> overlay of embroidery stitching across the entire surface of
> the quilt, I allow Mother Nature to add her own finishing
> touches . . . the fundamental design tricks of repetition
> and recurring themes help the garden retain a measure
> of visual unity – much as the quilter might use one color of
> thread to embroider many different patterns onto the
> quilt.[1]

A 'quilt garden' is a handy metaphor for describing the vari-
ation of Victorine personalities who make up the 'quilt' of
the Victorine abbey at Paris. On the surface the individual
Victorines to whom we now turn appear as a series of somewhat unrelated 'patches'. As we begin to explore them we
will see exegetes, theologians, contemplatives, liturgists, poets,
philosophers, metaphysicians, priests, spiritual teachers,
mystics, and subtle psychologists of the soul. They will speak
to us through a profusion of styles and genres. We will see
'literal' and 'spiritual' commentaries on Scripture, commentaries on early Christian fathers, guides for the contemplative
and moral life, mystical theology, philosophical theology, theological treatises and *summas*, catechisms and training
manuals for the novitiate, sermons, and didactic literature. We
will encounter a religious community passionate and varied
in its use of the imagination, symbols, allegory, the senses,
perception, experience, and reason. Various Victorines write of
the sacramental quality of the natural world and of history.
Others plumb the depths of psychological understanding of the
self and of the soul. Some speculate on the metaphysical
aspects and divine qualities of angels. All teach a life regulated
by and in God, Christ, the Spirit, and the Church.

Individual Victorines were as varied as the patches in a
quilt. Yet for all this wild variety, as with the 'quilt garden',
there were at St Victor unifying themes, borders, boundaries,
and patterns. These unifying 'threads' in the Victorine quilt
together comprise the Victorine spiritual tradition. But finally,
as the gardener allows Mother Nature to 'add the finishing
touches', so the Victorines acknowledged the gift of divine
grace as the final bond that unites the fecund tapestry of their
unique but inspirational practice of spirituality.

DOCTRINE AS DEVOTION

Compassionate charity and imaginative integration are two
threads woven into Victorine spirituality that have already
been pointed out. A third thread in the Victorine quilt stands

out. This thread represents the Victorine theme of integration between experience (grounded in the monastic mystical tradition) and critical reflection (at that time finding a new voice in the schools of Paris). The theme may be stated in a variety of ways. We might refer to this integration as the relation between 'theory and praxis', or 'theology and spiritual practice', or 'systematic theology and aesthetic theology', or 'dogmatic theology and mystical theology', or '*theoria* and *praktikos*',[2] or simply the 'active life and contemplative life'.

Contemporary writers are just now, however, beginning to recognize the incalculable loss initiated by the modern, post Victorine, separation of theology and spiritual practice.[3] A few examples of contemporary attempts to reunite theology and practice are illuminating.

One such writer speaks of 'mystical' and 'dogmatic' theologies that have a mutually enhancing influence on one another. This historical theologian states:

> The basis doctrines of the Trinity and Incarnation, worked out in these centuries, (through the late fifth century) are mystical doctrines formulated dogmatically. That is to say, mystical theology provides the context for direct apprehensions of God; while dogmatic theology attempts to incarnate those apprehensions in objectively precise terms that then, in their turn, inspire a mystical understanding of God.[4]

A well-known Christian philosopher speaks to the same issue when he says:

> We must cease to regard spiritual classics and the heart-stirring words of early theologians as merely "devotional" and not to be confused with theology or critical thinking. Rather than being occasionally stirred by devotional literature, we can actually become aware of God's presence everywhere, whether in academic theology or in our daily life.[5]

And one of our foremost contemporary writers on the subject

of the relation of history and theology to spirituality says simply and plainly:

> A theology that is alive is always grounded in spiritual experience. If it is to be complete, theology needs to be *lived* just as much as it needs to be studied and explained . . . The point of seeking doctrinal clarity is always to express, promote and protect a quite distinctive experience of God along with its practical implications for life and prayer.[6]

The Victorines *lived* and *practised* theology; doctrine *was* devotion. With this concept clearly in our minds as a primary theme or thread of Victorine spirituality, we can proceed to the Victorine masters themselves.

HUGH OF ST VICTOR (b. 1096 d. 1141)

Hugh of St Victor was the first great master of the order of Canons Regular at the house of St Victor in Paris. The most prolific of all Victorine writers, Hugh, with the possible exception of his student Richard of St Victor, was the most influential teacher to emerge from the Abbey of St Victor. Through his fame Hugh drew at least two generations of brilliant students of contemplation, theology, philosophy, and mysticism. His influence was felt throughout the medieval period and beyond, even to the contemporary revival of Christian spirituality. He is often called '*alter Augustinus*' due to his deep reliance on and astute interpretations of St Augustine whose practical teachings on contemplative life Hugh blended with the theoretical writings of Dionysius the Areopagite. Unlike some of his contemporaries, Hugh upheld secular learning by promoting such knowledge as an essential introduction to contemplative life: 'Learn everything,' he said, 'and you will see afterward that nothing is useless.' Some scholars have not hesitated to call him the most brilliant theologian of the entire twelfth century.

Born in 1096, most likely in Saxony, Hugh took the habit of

the Canons Regular of St Augustine at Hamerleve and later moved to Paris and St Victor's around 1115. He spent the rest of his life at St Victor's and was elected abbot in 1133 at which post he served until his death. Through the inspiration and guidance of Hugh, all Victorine writing reflects a healthy integration of contemplation, biblical exegesis, systematic and pastoral theology, preaching, catechesis, liturgy, and charity.

Hugh's works cover the whole range of the arts and sacred science taught in his day. A great mystical writer, he was also a philosopher and a scholastic theologian of the first order. Apparently he was a great lecturer, which accounts for his reputation and early dispersal of his works. His teaching was one of the foundations of Scholastic theology, and his influence has affected the whole development of Scholasticism. Hugh was also the leader of a great mystic movement of which the School of St Victor became the centre, and he formulated, as it were, a code of laws governing the soul's progress to union with God. The gist of his teaching is that knowledge is not an end in itself, but ought to be a stepping stone to the mystical life through thought, meditation, and contemplation. He is a true disciple of Augustine and Gregory the Great in his emphasis on the dynamic identity between introversion and ascension in the spiritual journey. In his work, *On the World's Vanity*, Hugh writes: 'To ascend to God is to enter into oneself, and not only to enter the self, but in an ineffable way to pass through oneself into the interior depths.'[7]

Hugh was no doubt the most comprehensive writer of the Victorines. If he did not reach the profundity of Richard's work on contemplation or the scope of Achard's sermons or the subtlety of Thomas Gallus' ability to balance love and knowledge in the ascent to God, he was none the less the one writer considered by St Bonaventure to possess authority equally in the areas of thinking, preaching and contemplation. Bonaventure says of Hugh:

> First one ought to labor at the study of doctrine, second the study of preaching, third the study of contemplation.

First it is best to study Augustine; second it is best to study Gregory, and third to study Dionysius. Anselm follows Augustine, Bernard follows Gregory, and Richard of St. Victor follows Dionysius; thus we follow Anselm in reasoning, Bernard in preaching, and Richard in contemplation. But truly, Hugh is master of all of these.[8]

Hugh's major works include the massive *On the Sacraments of the Christian Faith (De Sacramentis Christianae Fidei)*. This work deals with the knowledge of God and of the Trinity, sacramental theology, the restoration of creation and humanity through Christ, creation, angels, the Fall and its consequences, the sacraments, faith, incarnation, grace and the Church, the Eucharist, and more. It is considered by many to be the first scholastic *summa*. His *Didascalicon* serves as an outline for training Christian scholars in philosophy, spirituality, and theology, and as a methodological guide for reading Scripture. It is important for both his theological and mystical doctrines. Rising from visible things and visible symbols to the invisible things of God is an important theme for Hugh as it is for later Victorines. His thinking on this anagogic theme is treated most clearly in his *Commentary on the Celestial Hierarchy of Dionysius the Areopagite*. We will be looking more carefully at the importance of symbols in contemplation, theology, and ascent to God in later chapters.

Hugh's scriptural commentaries, which are important for his theological as well as mystical doctrines, include literal, allegorical, and tropological (moral) interpretations of the Pentateuch, the books of Kings, Ecclesiastes, Jeremiah, Joel, and the Song of Songs. His important mystical works include *On the Moral Ark of Noah (De arca Noe morali)*, *On the Mystical Ark of Noah (De arca Noe mystica)*, *On the Nature of Love (De substantia dilectionis)*, *On the Power of Praying (De virtuti orandi)*, *In Praise of Charity (De laude caritatis)*, and numerous homilies.

Through the inspiration and guidance of Hugh of St Victor, all Victorine writing reflects a healthy integration of the spiritual quest for self-understanding, for union with God, and for loving compassion for the world and for one's neighbour.

RICHARD OF ST VICTOR (d. 1173)

Richard of St Victor was the premier Victorine mystic, contemplative, and creative theologian. His writings on contemplation, union with God, and mystical theology had immense impact on Christian spirituality throughout the medieval period and beyond. He is the Victorine writer who, above any other, is destined to have the greatest impact on contemporary spiritual renewal. Dante said of him that he was 'in contemplation more than human' (*Paradiso* 11:132). And St Bonaventure recognized in Richard the 'modern' master of contemplation who equalled the greatest mystical writer among the fathers, Dionysius the Areopagite. It is Richard who more than any other exemplifies the Victorine awareness of the sacramental presence of God in nature, community, the human person, and the cosmos.

Apparently a native of Scotland, it is likely that Richard arrived at the Abbey of St Victor after the death of Hugh. Regardless of whether Richard knew Hugh personally, it is clear that Richard, in assimilating and transforming the best of Hugh's writing and wisdom, was deeply indebted to him. In matters of exegesis, theology, contemplation, and spirituality, Richard was deeply influenced by Hugh. Hugh built a foundation upon which Richard constructed the roof; Hugh added colour and thread to the tapestry of Latin spirituality upon which Richard wove ever more subtle patterns and hues. If Hugh was the flower of Victorine spirituality, Richard was its fragrance.[9]

Little is known of Richard's life. It is most likely that Richard came to Paris and the abbey at St Victor when he was a relatively young man, probably in the early 1150s. He seems to have transplanted well. Richard rose quickly to positions of authority, becoming Sub-prior in 1159 and Prior of St Victor's in 1162 until his death in 1173. Richard can be considered as the 'second generation' master of Victorine spirituality. Richard carries on the work begun by Hugh of a biblically based, liturgically sensitive, and theologically sophisticated spirituality. Utilizing imaginative allegory and intuitive reasoning he systematized a theory of mystical, contemplative theology drawing on Dionysius the Areopagite,[10] Augustine, Boethius, Gregory the Great, Eriugena, other twelfth-century spiritual writers, and of course Hugh. Under the influence of Dionysius the Areopagite especially, Richard of St Victor was able to integrate the apophatic or negative pathway of knowledge with the cataphatic or positive pathway of knowledge. This integration, along with his work on symbols and contemplation, influenced centuries of Christian spiritual writers.[11]

Richard of St Victor's writings are varied. His *Book of Selections* (*Liber Exceptionum*) is an encyclopaedic presentation of knowledge for training of novices rich in references to Patristic sources. Works that have made important contributions to the history of spirituality and which are currently available in English include the *Twelve Patriarchs* (often referred to as the *Benjamin Minor*) which, through the use of personification allegory, describes the preliminary stages of the life of virtue leading to contemplative awareness, the *Mystical Ark* (often referred to as the *Benjamin Major*) which systematizes Richard's insights on the grades or levels of contemplative consciousness, *On Elimination of Evil and Promotion of Good* on the life of virtue, meditation, and contemplation, and *On the Four Degrees of Passionate Charity* which sketches the itinerary of the 'path of love' leading to more perfect service of neighbour and, ultimately, union with God. Also available in partial translation are his *Mystical Notes on the Psalms* and Richard's great treatise on mystical theology, *On the Trinity*, which continues to influence writers on theology and spirituality even today. In *On the Trinity* Richard attempts to find in the human experience of love a basis for understanding the mystery of the Trinity. Other works include commentaries on the Psalms, the Song of Songs, the Apocalypse of John, theological works on the Holy Spirit and Christ, and numerous surviving sermons.

Four elements stand out in Richard's treatment of virtue and contemplation. The first element is his insistence that contemplation and ascent to God must be based on self-knowledge and personal discretion. A second is his pervasive Christological motif, while a third is that reason must be transcended or 'die' in order that the soul may enter the most intimate and divine mystery, the Trinity. A fourth element, also present in a number of other Victorine writers, is the oscillation in awareness between apparent oppositions. These oppositions include, among others, the darkness and the light that is God, or God's simultaneous absence or presence. These 'oscillations' carry the contemplative into the highest and most sublime mysteries of the Christian tradition – those of the humanity and divinity of Christ and of the unity in plurality of the Trinity.

It is, however, Richard of St Victor's *Mystical Ark* that represents the summit of twelfth-century contemplation and teaching. In the *Mystical Ark* Richard uses the symbol of the cherubim to communicate the highest forms of contemplation which he defines as 'the free penetration of the mind, hovering in wonder, into the varied manifestations of God's Wisdom' (*The Mystical Ark* 1.4). Richard also uses the Ark of the Covenant as a symbol of divine theophany, various elements of which symbolize six levels of spiritual and contemplative consciousness.

We will return to Richard of St Victor many times in the course of this book. He is indeed, as Dante said, 'in contemplation more than human'. A more precise analysis of Richard's writing on contemplation, however, would conclude that he advocates and teaches a practice of contemplation through which one becomes, not simply *more* than human, but rather *most* human.

THOMAS GALLUS (d. 1246) [THOMAS OF ST VICTOR, THOMAS OF VERCELLI]

Thomas Gallus, founder and abbot of the celebrated monastery of St Andrew at Vercelli, joins that remarkable group of medieval contemplatives, including Bernard of Clairvaux, Catherine of Siena, and Teresa of Avila who not only wrote about and practised mystical theology, but who were also involved in an intense and active life of political engagement. Though in residence at the Abbey of St Victor for but a short time, he remained throughout his life a Victorine in spirit, if not precisely in fact. A contemplative teacher and practitioner, Gallus none the less continued with the active administration and direction of the abbey and hospital at Vercelli throughout most of his life. He was known and revered from the thirteenth to the sixteenth centuries, primarily as a commentator on the Dionysian writings and as an exegete of the Song of Songs. However, from the seventeenth century until the early part of the twentieth century, Thomas Gallus (also known as Thomas of St Victor or Thomas of Vercelli) was largely forgotten. In recent years, he is being rediscovered.[12]

Thomas Gallus was born in France sometime shortly before 1200. He was teaching and writing in Paris by 1218, where he was a Canon at the abbey at St Victor. He later left Paris to found the Abbey of St Andrew at Vercelli in the Piedmont province of northern Italy. An indication of the effect of his writings and of his work as Prior and Abbot of St Andrew's is that, largely on Gallus' account, the Franciscans transferred their *studium generale* from Padua to Vercelli in 1228. However, Gallus' involvement in quarrels between popes and the Emperor Frederick II eventually forced him into exile in Ivrea in 1243, where he continued writing until his death in 1246.

Thomas Gallus' writings include three commentaries on the Song of Songs,[13] a *Commentary on Isaiah 6*, two mystical treatises, *On the Seven Grades of Contemplation* and *The Mirror of Contemplation*,[14] and two major works on the Dionysian corpus. These include *The Explanations*, an extended exposition, phrase by phrase, of the full Dionysian corpus, finished in 1243, and *The Extract*, finished in 1238.[15] Gallus' work gives evidence of the rich and deep tradition of devotion and contemplation in the Latin West. His complete corpus reflects the integration of monastic, metaphysical, theological, and spiritual themes as they developed within the Victorine spiritual tradition in particular and the Christian contemplative tradition in general. His work, along with Hugh and especially Richard of St Victor, serves to highlight the seminal work of Dionysius the Areopagite and its influence on subsequent centuries of Christian contemplative thought and practice.

ACHARD OF ST VICTOR (d. 1171)

It is surmised that Achard was born in England, but little is known of his early life. His presence at St Victor's, however, is firmly established in 1155 when he was elected abbot, following the successful abbacy of Gilduin. There is reason to believe that Achard was involved in the theological life of the Parisian schools. References to this life are mentioned in his sermons. Achard seems to have been a very effective administrator and was made Bishop of Avranches in 1161 where he served until his death in 1171.

In keeping with the general tone of Victorine spirituality, Achard practised the rhythm and integration of doctrine as devotion. In an introduction to recent translations of Achard's work into English, Hugh Feiss says of Achard that he 'makes no sharp distinction between theology, the pulpit, and meditation . . . like Hugh and Richard, Achard drew no sharp boundaries between the figurative, even playful use of theological imagination, as this had been cultivated in claustral settings since the early years of the Church, and the use of technical logic as this was being cultivated in the schools of Paris.'[16]

Achard's surviving works consist of fifteen sermons and two metaphysical treatises, *On the Distinction of the Soul, Spirit, and Mind* and *On the Unity of God and the Plurality of Creatures*. Three of the 'sermons' may be somewhat mislabelled. They are quite long and would take two to three hours if read aloud. The last of the sermons, *Sermon 15*, is in actuality a mystical tract on the contemplative life and is often referred to as *The Treatise on the Seven Deserts*. In this sermon, the human soul, having deserted God, becomes like a desert, a 'region of unlikeness' to God. But the soul begins to return to God through the action of Christ, symbolized by his forty-day stay in the desert. The sermon follows the soul through seven deserts in a journey that moves inward then upward to an ever greater intimacy and likeness to God. Achard says:

> O happy exchange! The human leaves the human and brings in God. How joyful and grateful a guest who fills the whole house he enters with grace and rejoicing. For a person to leave self for God's sake in this way is not to go out but to go in – not leaving the house for the vestibule, but for the bedchamber ... This is the divine will and reason: that you keep nothing of your self for yourself, so that when you have totally deserted yourself, the whole of God's will and reason will swell in you – to "adhere to God" and thus with him "to be one spirit."[17]

However, in the final desert, Achard joins so many other mystics in the Christian spiritual tradition as he moves naturally from deification into identification with Christ through compassionate service to neighbour.

Other important sermons include a discussion of Christ's 'nine transfigurations' which are meditations on the life of Christ concentrating not so much on historical details as on Christ's inner motivations and compassion (*Sermon 12*). *Sermon 13* is an extended discourse on the Christian's participation in Christ's three (trinitarian) attributes connected with the image of Christ as the master-builder who wishes to dwell in the house that Christ builds in us (*Sermon 13*). The sermon is an elaborate allegory using a house as an image of Christ's work of restoration. Achard ends this sermon by exclaiming,

'Oh house to be contemplated, Christ dwells in us in many ways, just as we participate in his fullness in many ways, above all in the way of virtue and discipline, in the way of sweetness and joy, and in the way of contemplation' (*Sermon 13.34*). At the end of Achard of St Victor's *On the Unity of God* he includes a tribute to Hugh's great theological synthesis, *On the Sacraments*, by referring to Hugh's distinction between God's two great works: the work of creation and the work of restoration. As his sermons and treatises show, Achard focused his contemplative attention on the mystery and process of Christ's saving and compassionate participation in the divine work of restoration.

ANDREW OF ST VICTOR (d. 1175)

Andrew of St Victor was a biblical exegete who became the foremost Victorine practitioner of interpretation by means of the 'literal' or 'historical' sense of Scripture. His intense commitment to the exposition of the literal sense even led him to the conclusion that this sense could be mined for its spiritual content. For Andrew, there was something transcendent even in the very words, historical events, and concrete details of Scripture. Andrew was most probably a pupil of Abbot Gilduin as well as Hugh of St Victor. He was no doubt a prior of St Victor when he was called to be abbot of a daughter house of St Victor located in the marshes at Wigmore, Wales. He left Wigmore in 1154 to return to St Victor's in Paris, only to return once again as abbot to Wigmore in 1163 where he died in 1175.

Andrew was a great admirer of Jewish exegetes, feeling always that he fell far behind them in their ability to interpret the Hebrew Scriptures. In Andrew, as Beryl Smalley has noted, we find a scholar in Paris who shows a total lack of interest in the work of theological speculation and synthesis that is blossoming all around him in the schools. He is instead independent, devoting himself to a relatively neglected branch of study suggested to him by his master, Hugh, the literal sense of Scripture. Andrew's exegetical method focuses primarily on expositions, not of whole texts, but of selected passages. In his exposition of the literal sense, he excludes the spiritual exposition on the one hand and theological questions on the other. He seldom addresses homiletics or doctrinal discussion.[18] Yet while this description of Andrew's character and writing may be true, one must take exception to Smalley's dismissal of Andrew's 'mystical' qualities. Andrew exemplifies what can be characterized as a spirituality of the intellectual life. In his pursuit of the literal sense, he expresses and presumably attempts to live according to an immediate consciousness of the presence of God found in the literal, historical meanings of Scripture. In that sense, Andrew was a mystic of the word.

Hugh had taught that to despise the literal sense was to despise the very ground of sacred literature. He said, for instance:

> If, as you say, we ought to leap straight from the letter to its spiritual meaning, then the metaphors and similes, which educate us spiritually, would have been included in the Scriptures by the Holy Spirit in vain. Do not despise what is lowly in God's word, for *by lowliness you will be enlightened to divinity*. The outward form of God's word seems to you, perhaps, like dirt, so you trample it underfoot, like dirt, and despise what the letter [i.e., literal sense] tells you was done physically and visibly. But hear! That dirt, which you trample, opened the eyes of the blind. Read Scripture then and first learn carefully what it tells you was done in the flesh.[19]

Andrew of St Victor carries Hugh's claim a step farther and insists on the possibility of finding a transcendent quality, even in the literal sense. Andrew uses the literal sense to become, in Hugh's words, *'enlightened to divinity'*. In his *Exposition on Ecclesiastes*, Andrew justifies literal inquisitiveness as a means to search out that which is hidden:

> He [the Preacher of Ecclesiastes] calls enquiry and research "this worst occupation" because much labor

brings little progress therein. He says that God hath given it to the children of men, to be exercised therein because of God's gift, the soul, whose natural instinct is to seek and search out concerning all things, that she may as it were pursue and capture the hidden fugitive, truth, with what speed she can; for all truth is hidden.[20]

If Richard of St Victor sought the hidden truth in allegorical, anagogical, and tropological interpretations of Scripture, Andrew of St Victor sought a similar truth in the literal or historical sense of the Hebrew Bible. Both men follow in the footsteps of their master, Hugh of St Victor. Andrew's contribution is that he makes the 'literal' sense a proper subject for study in itself. He seeks to understand the literal meaning of Scripture exactly as possible in order to visualize the biblical scene or narrative. In this way he continues the great tradition of the spiritual practice of *lectio divina* by entering more deeply and immediately into meditation upon Scripture.

In his exposition of the literal sense of the Hebrew Bible, Andrew of St Victor was in many ways a spiritual voyager unique to his time. In his *Prologue* to *The Exposition of Ezekiel* Andrew speaks both as a fearless explorer accepting God as guide and yet, reading between the lines, a somewhat beleaguered, lonely, and anxious exegete: 'With God as leader, who makes ways in the sea, paths in the stormy water, we take our way unfearing through unknown, pathless places, no end in sight.'[21]

ADAM OF ST VICTOR (d. 1146)

Adam was educated at Paris and entered the Abbey of St Victor when he was quite young, about 1133. In Paris, Adam worked with many influential figures, including Peter Abelard and Hugh of St Victor. As a poet and composer, Adam's greatest contribution is as the author of a large number of liturgical sequences, many of which survive.[22] He is often considered the most illustrious example of the revival of liturgical poetry of the twelfth century and is credited with perfecting the style of imagistic rhythmic poetry that became the hallmark of medieval sequences. Close study of both texts and music show that the Victorines were the first major contributors to the liturgical sequence repertory. The texts of all Adam's works reveal not only a defence of Victorine theological positions, but also imaginative and sophisticated use of biblical imagery, and an exegesis related to the ideals established by Hugh of St Victor.

GODFROY [GODEFROID] OF ST VICTOR (d. 1194)

An appreciative and devoted disciple of Hugh and Richard of St Victor, Godfroy came to the Abbey between 1150 and 1155 after prolonged literary and philosophical studies elsewhere. During a short exile from St Victor Godfroy wrote *The Fountain of Philosophy (Fons philosophiae)*, a poetic account of the seven liberal arts and theology which is also partly autobiographical and throws light on the people and customs of the scholastic world of the day. His important work, *Microcosmus*, is a commentary on the six days of creation that focuses on the correlative relation between the human soul as microcosm and the created world as macrocosm. In this work Godfroy shows the thought patterns of a humanist: nature is good, humanity in unfallen condition is good and after the redemption becomes capable of every excellence. In his works Godfroy insists that the gifts of grace perfect the gifts of nature, that the body and soul are indissolubly united and form one being. As with a number of the other Victorines, he focuses on the ascent of the soul from lower, visible things to higher, invisible things. He does not present a theoretically ordered mystical theology of love and knowledge as do most of the Victorine masters. He is in accord, however, with Richard, Thomas, and Achard in finding love, as it imitates the selfless love of Christ, to be the highest human achievement.

WALTER OF ST VICTOR [WALTHER] (d. 1180)

Little is known of Walter of St Victor except that around 1175 he was Prior of St Victor and that he died in about the year 1180. In addition to a few sermons on Mary and Jesus, he is best known for his polemic *Against the Four Labyrinths of France (Contra quatuor labyrinthos Franciae)*. The 'Four Labyrinths' against whom Walter wrote were Abelard, Gilbert de la Porrée, Peter Lombard, and Peter of Poitiers. It is a bitter attack on the dialectical method in theology, and condemns in no measured terms the use of logic in explanation of the mysteries of the faith. Walter is incensed at the thought of treating the Trinity and incarnation with what he calls 'scholastic levity.' In doing so he discards the best traditions of Hugh, Richard, Achard, and the majority of other Victorine masters as he pours abuse on these philosophers, theologians, and grammarians. His vehemence and bile, however, defeated his purpose, which was to discredit the dialecticians. Not only did he fail to convince his contemporaries, but he probably also hastened the triumph of the method he attacked. Four years after his work was published, the Pope made Peter of Poitiers, one of the 'labyrinths', chancellor of the Diocese of Paris. Before the end of the century another 'labyrinth', Peter Lombard, was recognized as a primary authority in theology. Lombard's methods were adopted and used in the schools and his *Sentences* became a standard medieval text.

The Victorine school of spirituality, taken as a whole, promulgated and practised the integration of all aspects of the religious life. In this chapter we have characterized this propensity toward unification of disciplines by the phrase: 'doctrine as devotion'. This conscious integration on the part of the Victorines serves as a compelling model of the spiritual life for our contemporary search for spiritual renewal.

2. MAPPING THE SPIRITUAL JOURNEY

> However far you go, you will never find the boundaries of the soul.
>
> Heraclitus, Greek, 6th–5th century BCE

In the *Didascalicon* Hugh of St Victor notes the prerequisites for attaining wisdom. These include humility, hard work, a peaceful life, silent meditation, poverty, and a foreign land. Of the latter Hugh writes:

> It is, therefore, a great source of virtue for the practiced mind to learn, bit by bit, to change concerning visible and transitory things, so that afterwards it may be able to leave them behind altogether. The person who finds their homeland sweet is still a tender beginner; the one to whom every soil is as their native soil is already strong; but that one is perfect to whom the entire world is as a foreign land. The tender soul has fixed their love on one spot in the world; the strong soul has extended its love to all places; the perfect soul has extinguished her love [of place altogether]. From boyhood I have dwelt on foreign soil.[1]

In *Sermon 15* Achard of St Victor speaks of exile in a similar way, and in fact all the canons at St Victor abandoned their homeland for the sake of wisdom and Christ. They pursued a physical or outer journey from home for the sake of a better home. This outer journey which, as Hugh describes, moves from love of place to love of all things to detachment from all worldly things for the sake of love of Wisdom (read 'Christ' or 'God'), is echoed by an inner journey. This inner journey is the spiritual journey of the soul into God. Not only did the

Victorines find correspondences between our outer and inner spiritual journeys; they were also masters in mapping out dynamic routes by which the soul might make progress toward and into God.

Many commentators have noted the Victorine trait of systematizing the spiritual ascent or journey. On the surface these 'maps' of the journey may at times seem static. After all, how can one systematically map a route into what is essentially beyond the confines of any system: the boundless mystery of God? But in the context of the new spiritual consciousness of the twelfth century, these maps of the spiritual journey are anything but static. They are dynamic and transformative 'outlines' of the soul's journey into God that depict spiritual growth, formation, and development. They seek out Hugh's 'foreign exile' in that they move from the familiar to the unfamiliar, from regions of likeness and similitude to regions of unlikeness, dissimilitude, and unknowing. In doing so they employ a range of spiritual strategies. These include the use of visual and allegorical exegesis, the deployment of symbolic theology, the invention of imaginative metaphors, a metaphysics of anagogical lifting up to the invisible things of God by means of the visible things of the world, and the creative use of sacramental symbols drawn from the natural world, the self, Scripture, and liturgy.

Victorine maps of the spiritual journey thus come to us as dynamic and developmental 'outlines' of the journey into God. At times these spiritual maps or models of the journey of the soul into God are linear in movement as in the simple progression from purgation, to illumination, to union as first described, for instance, by Dionysius the Areopagite. At other times these Victorine patterns become more complex and take on more of the nature of circular, even spherical movement that anticipates Teresa of Avila's 'interior castles'. Often an apparent linear model turns back upon itself in a kind of spiral pattern that guides the soul into ever deeper levels of conscious awareness of world, self, and God. The spiralling loops of this pattern, however, never reach into the absolute depths that are the mystery of God. Rather, with each loop, they descend (or we could equally say 'ascend') ever deeper into divine mystery while at the same time never completely exhausting that mystery. This latter spiral pattern is reminiscent of Gregory of Nyssa's *epektasis,* where each divine encounter only serves to lead one into ever deeper understanding and love. But regardless of this diversity of 'pattern' in these maps of the individual's spiritual journey into that divine 'foreign land', there are a number of constants that suggest their Victorine origin: they are forged in community, inspired by tradition, grounded in the great spiritual awakening of the twelfth century, and have as their goal union with God and connection, through compassion, with all creation. Victorine maps of the spiritual journey would continue to have enormous influence on spiritual understanding and practice for centuries to come.

VICTORINE INTEGRATION: A REMINDER FOR THE SPIRITUAL JOURNEY

Before we begin to look at a variety of Victorine maps of the spiritual journey we need to remind ourselves of the Victorine propensity to integrate disciplines. Again, for the Victorines, their spirituality, theology, exegesis, preaching, prayer and con-templation, intuitive or metaphorical imagination, and compassionate charity were of a piece. It is no different when we look at their maps of the soul's journey into God. When we examine, for instance, Richard of St Victor's *Twelve Patriarchs* we are looking at a work that is simultaneously biblical exegesis, theology, a depiction of the life of virtue, allegory, sacramental cosmology, and teaching on levels of mystical con-sciousness by a master of the practice of contemplation. We will examine many of these key elements of the composition of Victorine maps of the spiritual journey in later chapters of this book as appropriate. But it will help to look briefly at a few of these aspects of Victorine spirituality now, before we accompany them on their spiritual journey.

Many of the elements that effect Victorine spirituality are

derived from the fifth- or sixth-century work of Dionysius the Areopagite. Dionysius was one of the first Christian mystics to write of the spiritual journey in terms of the dynamic process of purification, illumination, and union or perfection. Dionysius expresses this process in a number of places within his corpus, but one expression is especially interesting in that it also alludes to the angels of the angelic hierarchy as objects of imitation in the soul's quest for God. Victorines including Richard, Hugh, and Thomas Gallus explore the angelic hierarchy as models of the human spiritual journey into virtue and contemplation. Dionysius had said:

> Indeed for every member of the [celestial, that is the angelic] hierarchy, perfection consists in this, that it is uplifted to imitate God as far as possible and, more wonderful still, that it becomes what scripture calls a "fellow worker for God" (1 Cor. 3:9) and a reflection of the workings of God. Therefore when the hierarchical order lays it on some to be purified and others to do the purifying, on some to receive illumination and on others to cause illumination, on some to be perfected and on others to bring about perfection, each will actually imitate God in the way suitable to whatever role it has.[2]

Dionysius also refers to the angels being 'uplifted' to imitate God. In Victorine writing this 'uplifting' is referred to as anagogy which can be defined as any process by which the mind or soul is 'elevated' into God. Symbols of all kinds are important in Victorine spirituality because they aid in the anagogical process. Symbols utilize the visible things of the world as 'signposts' to invisible things. Anagogy and symbol are in turn intimately related to apophatic (or negative) and cataphatic (or positive) method. Anagogy has a slightly apophatic connotation while symbol has a slightly cataphatic connotation. These relations can sometimes become confusing but will be explained clearly in Chapters Three and Five. Part of the confusion stems from the fact that the terms 'apophatic' and 'cataphatic' are used to describe types of spirituality, modes of prayer, paths to God, and theological method.

Regardless of this potential for confusion, two things are clear in the Victorine use of the apophatic and cataphatic way: (1) they are based on a conception of the sacred and sacramental quality of the created world, and (2) following the lead of Dionysius, they insist on balancing the relative value of the apophatic and cataphatic ways of knowing. Thus in the spiritual journey, the Victorines are concerned with both the absence (apophatic nature) of God *and* the presence (cataphatic nature) of God. The same can be said about the paths of darkness and light, the way of images in contemplation and the way of self-emptying in contemplation, the journey into God by means of God's divine names and the journey into God by means of God's essential mystery or incomprehensibility. All of these are balanced and based on a sacramental cosmology. Though individual Victorines often show a preference, taken as a whole Victorine spirituality does not, as a rule, value one path over and against the other.

One scholar explains the Dionysian view:

> Affirmation and negation in Pseudo-Dionysius are not mutually exclusive options to be exercised separately . . . The Areopagite carefully preserved the simultaneity of procession and return, and thus of affirmation and negation. A given expression or symbol about God is denied because of its ultimate dissimilarity, but it is also and at the same time, affirmed because of its relative similarity.[3]

And so too, within Victorine writing on the spiritual journey, is this simultaneity of affirmation and negation carefully maintained.

Hugh and Richard of St Victor inherit from Dionysius both the anagogic use of symbols and the basic structure of symbols as moving, in the famous Victorine phrase, *per visibilia ad invisibilia* – 'through the visible things [of the world] to the invisible things [both created (angels) and uncreated (God)].'

In his commentary *On the Apocalypse of John*, Richard of St Victor defines symbol and anagogy as:

> Beyond the illuminating rays of the most sacred eloquence, when it is possible, we look upon the manifestation of heavenly souls by means of symbols and anagogy. The symbol is the gathering together of visible forms to demonstrate invisible things. Anagogy is the ascension or elevation of the mind contemplating the highest things.[4]

Hugh of St Victor also focuses on the anagogic use of symbols defining symbol as 'a juxtaposition, that is, a joining together of visible forms set forth to demonstrate invisible things.'[5] Hugh of St Victor's *Commentary* on the *Celestial Hierarchy* of Denys the Areopagite is, in major part, a treatise on symbols and how they function in contemplation and in the anagogical journey into God. Thomas Gallus also emphasizes the use of symbols that lead from the visible to the invisible. In Gallus' case the angels, along with Jesus, Scripture, and the tradition of the Fathers, are 'symbols' that lead the soul back to God. Gallus writes that:

> Just as the Lord Jesus himself first inwardly illuminated us, let us then, according to our ability, look upon the anagogic illuminations of the sacred Scriptures handed down by the holy Fathers. Afterwards, let us contemplate, according as we are able, the angelic hierarchies manifested to us by the illuminations themselves as anagogical signs.[6]

For the Victorines all creation is a potential symbol that can function anagogically, in effect lifting the soul into awareness of divine presence. Symbols are entry points into deeper levels of meaning, into deeper levels of spiritual awareness. But it would be wrong to think of the contemplative anagogy of these spiritual journeys as disengaged from the body or out of touch with the natural world. For the Victorines the soul is restored to Truth as a concrete 'thing' (*res*) intimately integrated with an 'image' (*imago*). This, in fact, is a Christological truth: the restoration of the humble 'thing' and the victorious 'image' is the restoration of the flesh and the spirit in Christ.

Once again then, and in this case in the context of the spiritual journey, it is essential that we view Victorine writing as a tapestry. In the following examples we will find an elegant Victorine tapestry woven from narrative symbols drawn from spiritual as well as moral interpretations of Scripture, processes of purification, the dynamics of holiness, structures of mental faculties, modes and sequences of spiritual experiences, mystical states of awareness, categories of divine revelation, compassionate action and more. Often, as noted above, in these maps of the spiritual journey the structurally defining image is from a biblical narrative interpreted symbolically. Because of this dynamic complexity, Victorine outlines of the spiritual life are recognizable even today as accurate guides for interpreting our own spiritual experience and journey.

RICHARD OF ST VICTOR: TWELVE STAGES OF THE SPIRITUAL LIFE

Richard of St Victor is justly famous for his complex personification allegory of the twelve stages of spiritual awareness and discipline in *The Twelve Patriarchs*. In this work biblical characters connected in an historical narrative depict a sequence of events in the external world that become symbolic of a sequence in the inner life of a person. Two biblical narratives are involved in this map of the spiritual journey. The first is the story of the birth of twelve sons – the twelve patriarchs – and one daughter to Jacob, his two wives and their two handmaidens. The second narrative is of the disciples' experience of Jesus' transfiguration. The treatise is interpreted according to one of the 'spiritual' senses of Scripture, that of the 'tropological' or moral sense. Drawing together Jacob, his two wives, their handmaidens, and their children, Richard defines not only a system of moral progress, but also a whole epistemology, a complete allegory of the human person. The allegory reveals how the affective and intellectual powers of the soul are to be trained in order to attain contemplation.

In the complex structure of the *Twelve Patriarchs,* Jacob, or 'Israel' (that is, 'the one who sees God') represents the 'rational soul'.[7] His two wives represent the principle powers of the soul. Rachel is 'reason'; Leah is 'affection', which includes will, emotion, and sensibility. These allegories echo the standard medieval allegories of Rachel representing the contemplative life and Leah representing the active life. Rachel, as reason, leads to all truth; Leah as affection leads to all virtue: truth and virtue in Victorine spiritual teaching are intimately connected. Rachel's handmaiden Bilhah represents the imagination which links reason to the world of perception. Leah's handmaiden is Zilpah who represents the five bodily senses that connect affection with the external world. In these allegories Richard outlines his concept of the mind and will in relation to self and world. The grouping of Jacob's children to the mothers is also significant. The groups represent successive stages in the contemplative quest. The children of Leah are the virtues that discipline the will; those of Bilhah govern thought; Zilpah's children control deeds; and Rachel's represent the life of asceticism and signify contemplation. Taken together, the sons of Jacob represent the twelve stages of the spiritual life.

With *The Twelve Patriarchs* Richard of St Victor adds depth of psychological insight and subtle clarity to the dynamic process of spiritual formation and growth. The culmination of this portion of the spiritual journey is contemplation (Richard takes us deeper into the stages and modes of contemplation in the *Mystical Ark* or *Benjamin Major*). Contemplation is born when Rachel (reason) dies in giving birth to Benjamin, whose identification with ecstatic contemplation is based on Psalm 67:27–28. Rachel's death at the birth of Benjamin is symbolic of a basic truth of contemplative ecstasy: it transcends all reasoning. Reason is, in a sense, dead when ecstasy occurs. The overall scheme of *The Twelve Patriarchs* can be outlined as follows:

Leah: (*affections*) Ordered Affections; Virtues Governing the Will
>   1. **Reuben**: Humility; Distance Between Creator and Creature
>   2. **Simeon**: Grief
>   3. **Levi**: Hope through Forgiveness
>   4. **Judah**: Love of Justice; Love of God

Bilhah: Rachel's maid (*imagination*)
>   5. **Dan**: Literal Use of Images
>   6. **Naphtali**: Use of Visual Things to Represent Invisible, Spiritual Truths

Zilpah: Leah's maid (*discipline of the senses*)
>   7. **Gad**: Abstinence
>   8. **Asher**: Patience

Leah: (*affections*) Second Group
>   9. **Issachar**: Joy of Interior Sweetness
>   10. **Zebulun**: Hatred of Vices
>   **Dinah**: Shame (Crisis in Ascetic Life; Distortions of Spiritual Disciplines)
>   Rape by Shechem: (Pride and Egotism)
>   Shechem Murdered by Simeon and Levi: (Inept Spiritual Guidance)

Rachel: (*reason*)
>   11. **Joseph**: Full Self-knowledge
>   12. **Benjamin**: Contemplation in Ecstasy

Reuben, as humility or 'fear of God', is the first step in Richard's scheme of the spiritual journey. This is not fear in the sense of punishment, guilt, or shame, but in the sense of humility based on the knowledge of the distinction between God as Creator and humanity as created. Joseph's birth represents the culmination of discipline through full self-knowledge. He also personifies the ordering and moderating function of reason in relation to the virtues. Between the births of Joseph and Benjamin an important transition takes place. The transition is one from shared human initiative with divine response to a situation of grace alone. Benjamin's ecstatic contemplation is a gift, a divine revelation or 'showing' that emphasizes the process of unveiling spiritual truths that are otherwise hidden. Richard utilizes metaphors of light to emphasize the revelatory gift of these divine 'showings'.

The mention of light brings Richard to a new representation: that of the mountain of Jesus' transfiguration. For Richard, the transfiguration represents four stages in the experience of contemplation.[8] The first is the climb up the mountain, 'a steep way, a secret way, unknown to many' signifying the long period of discipline represented by Jacob's first twelve children. In the second, a stage of detachment, the disciples (representing work, meditation, and prayer) remain with Jesus on the mountain, indicating stability, inner peace, and quiet. The third stage is the transfiguration itself where Jesus is clothed in light, reflecting, as did the transition between the births of Joseph and Benjamin, movement from human initiative into divine grace. Unlike many other writers on the journey of the soul into God, Richard gives a positive role to visions of light between the important transitional stages of internal quiet and recollection and that of contemplation. In the fourth and final stage the disciples fall senseless to the ground when they hear the voice of God echoing from a brilliant cloud. The fainting of the disciples, echoing the earlier death of Rachel as 'reason', represents the failure of sense, memory, and reason at the highest levels of contemplation.

The Twelve Patriarchs ends with the allegories of the transfiguration and the birth of Benjamin. In both cases Richard hints at additional stages in the spiritual journey. These additional 'stages' of the grades and modes of contemplation 'above and beyond' reason are those that he will explore in detail in the *Mystical Ark,* arguably the most important and influential mystical work to come out of the abbey at St Victor.

THOMAS GALLUS: THE NINE ANGELIC ORDERS AS SPIRITUAL PATHS

Christian mystics and spiritual writers as diverse as Ambrose, Jerome, Dionysius the Areopagite, Gregory the Great, John Scotus Eriugena, and other writers into the twelfth century and beyond have used angelic orders as symbols and theophanies of spiritual paths into God. For these writers, the celestial hierarchy, almost universally composed of nine angelic orders, is a comprehensive, mandalic map of the spiritual journey. Thomas Gallus, in his *Prologue* to the *Commentary on the Song of Songs*, assimilates and modifies this tradition.[9] His modifications use the celestial hierarchy as an analogue to the human soul. Gallus develops, as it were, an angelic hierarchy of the soul with each angelic order corresponding to a grade or level of spiritual consciousness. This angelic anthropology, as we might call it, clarifies how we experience God and helps us to visualize and practise the most intimate knowledge of God. And, according to Gallus, as the angels themselves clarify, call us to imagine, and teach their unique paths to God, we become more human and at the same time more Godlike through them.

It must be emphasized, however, that for all these writers, including Thomas Gallus, the angels themselves do not represent the most comprehensive route to God. The angels are mediators between humanity and God, but they are not the Mediator.[10] Christ alone is *the* Mediator. As Gallus says elsewhere:

> It is through the careful consideration of the blessed, beautiful and wounded Christ. For among all the mind's exercises for the ascent of the spiritual intelligence, this is the most efficacious. Indeed, the more ardent we are in his most sweet love, through devout and blessed imaginative gazing upon him, the higher shall we ascend in the apprehension of the things of the Godhead.[11]

None the less, for Gallus this mediating activity of Christ is reflected to us through the diverse activity within the angelic orders that represent the many ways and forms of seeing God.

Much of the writing in the Latin West concerning the angelic orders as spiritual paths into God is grounded in Dionysius the Areopagite's *Celestial Hierarchy*. Dionysius focuses on nine angelic orders of which he says that the seraphim, cherubim, and thrones are 'in immediate proximity to God'; the dominions, powers, and authorities are in 'complete conformity to God'; and the principalities, archangels and angels participate in 'divine revelations to the world'. Gallus uses these same nine orders of angels as analogues of the human soul, developing 'angelic hierarchies of the human soul' correlated to each of the nine orders. Each angelic order thus manifests its particular attribute while at the same time modelling a spiritual path into God. As humans we have the opportunity to imitate or to contemplate a particular attribute of some angelic order, while at the same time pursuing the particular spiritual path reflected by that order.

Gallus' nine ways of 'seeing' God were based on the attributes of each angelic order as follows:

Angelic Order	Attribute/Spiritual Wisdom	Pathway to God
Angels	Balanced Use of Knowledge and Love	Messengers of Knowledge and Love to Others
Archangels	Appropriate Use of Knowledge	Discerning Judgement and Love
Principalities	Flight from Evil and Attention to Good	Guide Lower Orders to Divine Light
Powers	Discernment Between Good and Evil	Desire to Seek the Highest Good
Virtues	Correct Course of Action Leading to Virtue	Resolution to Follow Path of Virtue to Good
Dominions	Authentic Exercise of Free Will	'Sober' Use of Mind Extended to Highest Rays of Divine Intellect
Thrones	Ecstasy of Mind Open to Divine Light	Total Receptivity to Divine Visitation

| Cherubim | Death of Intellect | Union with Good in 'Unknowing' |
| Seraphim | Brilliant Radiance and Fiery Ardour of Love | Highest Love Uniting Soul to God; Receive and Pass On Flood of Divine Light |

Obviously Gallus sees each of the hierarchies as reflecting some portion of the divine light. Some reflect the life of virtue, others the power to discern good from evil, and still others the path of knowledge. Each in its turn sheds its own special portion of divine reality in succession through all the lower orders. According to Gallus, through the grace of God and as a kind of ontological chemistry of the soul, we may imitate and follow the angels into new depths of spiritual awareness. And there can be no doubt that the seraphim, circling in intimate proximity to God, reflect the pathway that leads most deeply into God: the path of love and compassionate charity.

HUGH OF ST VICTOR: TWELVE STAGES OF CONTEMPLATIVE ASCENT

In following Hugh of St Victor's stages of contemplative ascent in his two treatises on Noah's Ark, *On the Moral Ark of Noah* and *On the Mystical Ark of Noah*, we are once again confronted with the confluence of theology, exegesis, and contemplation in Victorine writing on the spiritual journey.

An intriguing aspect of Hugh of St Victor's work in these treatises is his insight into the necessity of 'awakening' to the spiritual journey. As we have seen, the classic trichotomy of stages in the growth of spiritual awareness had been purgation, illumination, union/perfection. Hugh recognizes the necessity of 'awakening' to spiritual awareness. Without 'awakening' to the potential for more intimate contact with divinity, there would certainly be no effort or even knowledge of the stages that follow. We need to 'wake up' to the presence of God.

Hugh presents the contemplative 'steps in the ascents, whereby we climb to heaven', as a series of twelve steps or degrees, arranged in four groups of three stages each.[12] These four stages represent the broad outline of the restoration of humanity, since the contemplative quest is essentially one of retracing the path by which humanity has fallen away from God. The ascension of the contemplative in the spiritual journey is a return to that state of love and knowledge of God in which humanity was created. The stages are presented as remedies for the three vices of the Fall: pride, ignorance, and concupiscence. The fourth stage is not a flight from vice but an advance in virtue, from the good into compassion. Each stage is accessible only through the power of Christ, whose activity is symbolically represented through the images of the 'tree of life' and the 'book of life'. The stages and grades are as follows:

Awakening (Christ's Role: The Book that Corrects)

Ascent from Pride:	Fear
	Grief
	Love

Purgation (Christ's Role: The Tree that Shades)

Ascent from Concupiscence:	Patience
	Mercy
	Compunction

Illumination (Christ's Role: The Book that Illumines)

Ascent from Ignorance:	Cognition
	Meditation
	Contemplation

Perfection/Union (Christ's Role: The Tree that Nourishes)

Ascent from Good to Compassion:	Temperance
	Prudence
	Fortitude

As with Richard of St Victor's *Mystical Ark*, Hugh's stages of the contemplative quest represent the gradual building of the divine dwelling-place in the human heart. The process is, one might say, the construction or 'painting' of an internal icon, the temple within, accessible and available to the contemplative on a journey toward God at any time and any place. The grades of ascent also illustrate once again the fundamental Victorine insight that virtue and knowledge are inseparable, being but two aspects of the same quest. The three levels of the state of illumination compose one of the most famous Victorine triads: cognition, meditation, and contemplation. We will encounter this triad as we look more closely at Victorine contemplation.

Grover Zinn has noted, regarding these two treatises, that Hugh seems to have been drawn to the ark of Noah by the fact that it floats upon the chaotic waters of the Flood. In this sense, the ark becomes an allegorical and tropological symbol of a point of stability in the moving flux of time and in the chaotic conflict of desires engendered by the love of the world. The divine plan for the salvation of humankind is achieved in the process of building a spiritual ark in which humanity escapes the flood of this world. In the works of restoration, God institutes the Church, the allegorical Ark, into which the faithful of every generation are gathered for their pilgrimage through this world to their celestial haven.[13]

ACHARD OF ST VICTOR: THE SEVEN DESERTS

In an ancient tradition tracing its roots to Augustine, humanity, on the one hand, bears a certain 'likeness' to God, an image of its Creator, yet on the other hand it dwells in a region of 'unlikeness', a region deformed and rendered unlike God through sin. The first 'likeness' is the basis of the doctrine of the *imago Dei*. The second 'unlikeness' results in uneasy wandering, called by Latin writers *peregrinatio,* which is the root of our word for the most swift and wide-ranging birds of prey, the peregrine falcon. Our dwelling in this region of 'unlikeness' is the genesis of Augustine's famous phrase: 'our hearts are restless until they find rest in Thee.' Achard of St Victor utilizes and reshapes this tradition by reformulating the concept of 'unlikeness' into the metaphor of the desert, describing a passage through seven deserts which brings the soul to ever greater intimacy and, ironically, 'likeness' to God.

Among the Victorines, Achard is particularly adept at

depicting the spiritual life as a series of stages. His *Sermon
12* 'On the Transfiguration of the Lord' illustrates the spiritual
journey by means of the nine transfigurations of the Lord
paying particular attention to the complicated interplay
between the soul and the body in the final transformations.
Sermon 13, which we will look at in detail in a later chapter,
presents an elaborate allegory of the spiritual life based upon
the construction of the 'house built upon the rock'. This allegory moves through the life of virtue into contemplation and
touches on elements of the journey affecting mind, body,
and spirit. In all of his allegories of the spiritual journey the
end of the journey, our salvation, coalesces with the journey's
beginning in such a way as to preclude an understanding of
the spiritual journey as a rigid sequence of steps. For Achard,
faith, hope, desire, the intellect, and love are operative
throughout the journey, insuring a dynamic but infinitely
varied process of spiritual growth.

Sermon 15 describes the journey through the 'seven deserts'.
The 'deserts' are those regions of 'unlikeness' to God through
which we must traverse to unite with Christ and attain full
love of God and neighbour. Achard's desert sermon can be
outlined as follows:

Seven Deserts:
1. Desert of Sin
2. Desert of the World
3. Desert of the Flesh
4. Desert of Self-will
5. Desert of Reason
    Interlude One: The Dwelling Place of Unction and
    Delight
    Interlude Two: The Heaven of Angels and Contem-
    plation of Eternal Reasons
6. Desert of the Spiritual Generation of the Son of God
7. Desert of Complete Identification with Christ

The first five deserts must be submitted to a process of 'purification' and can be abandoned one after the other. As a result,

proper order is restored: universe and humanity coalesce, the flesh, senses, and will are integrated, and reason is submitted to God. Through this process interior peace is achieved. The sermon is based on Matthew 4:1: 'Jesus was led by the Spirit into the desert.' The final two deserts focus on the contemplative life. The land of promise, reached by crossing many deserts, is situated in the interior of each human person. Those who have wandered off into the land of 'unlikeness' *return to the land of promise by returning to themselves.* Thus, as with Hugh of St Victor, the first deserts are deserts of 'awakening' to self.

The first five deserts comprise Achard's ascetical teaching concerning the journey of the soul to God. They may be taken together to comprise the 'active life'. The final two deserts, taken together represent the 'contemplative life'. The distinction between these two lives is somewhat artificial, however. Achard says that, like Mary and Jesus, we are called to possess the fullness of both the active and the contemplative life. Achard inserts two 'interludes' between deserts five and six. In the first, he introduces devotion as an intermediate state between active and contemplative living. Hugh Feiss defines devotion in Achard as 'a feeling or sentiment *(affectus)*, inseparable from prayer, which turns a person toward God, and with charity attaches the soul, detached from exterior things, to God. Devotion is an affective seizing of the divine reality, which the spirit does not yet see but already feels to be very near. It engenders delight.'[14] In the second interlude, delight in unction raises the soul to contemplation, which in turn engenders even greater delight. Of contemplation Achard says, 'I judge the eagle in the sky is the soul snatched from the snare of the body by contemplation and freely suspended in God as though upon intellectual wings.'[15]

With the sixth and seventh desert Achard enters fully into the realm of contemplation. Achard moves from a mystical union in the sixth desert to identification with Christ in the seventh. The result is that, paradoxically, in an abandonment of self and world for God, one identifies finally with Christ which, in imitation of Christ's humanity, necessitates in turn an 'abandonment' of God for love of neighbour. To go out from oneself, Achard says, makes it possible to return to oneself: 'They leave . . . from themselves into God, so that God comes into them and they come into God.' This mystical union Achard describes as *excessus mentis* (most likely derived from Richard of St Victor), as divinization, and as reformation in the form of God. Both heart and mind approach this union, but it is love itself that reaches into the very heart of the divine mystery.[16]

It is only for those who have first deserted their neighbour for God that the seventh desert, the desertion of God for neighbour, pertains. In the seventh desert God is deserted for the humanity of Christ, giving the contemplative a new view of earthly life from Christ's perspective. Here the contemplative sees the misery of human beings, and wishes that others could be as they are. They remember the example of Christ, who emptied himself to be among human beings, for human beings, as a human being. The contemplative longs simply to rest with Christ, but with all Christian mystics obtaining identity with the humanity of Christ, such rest is impossible. The very love that drew Christ from heaven to earth draws them, causing them to 'desert' God for the human good. In this seventh desert:

> The trajectory Achard traces is not from the humanity of Christ to his divinity, but from his humanity to his divinity, to his humanity in an endless loop. The perfect love that Christ possesses by grace in his humanity is and ever will be that in which we participate, and by which we participate in divine life. We will never cease to be drawn toward one another by the cords of love, which drew the Son of God to become our brother.[17]

The seven deserts, as was mentioned earlier, are not a simple, linear sequence of spiritual advancement. At the end of his sermon, Achard speaks of the alternation between night and day, between tribulation and consolation, even for those who have traversed all deserts. In this life, perfection, if there is perfection at all, returns upon itself, requiring constant reaffirmation and renewal. In abandoning God for love of neighbour in the seventh desert through identification with Christ, one finds oneself once again in the world and in the midst of sin. Thus one must once again enter into the first desert to confront and desert the reality of sin.[18] But we have our small graces. In every desert God's angels minister consolation, just at they did to Christ during his forty days in the desert.

TEACHING, EXPERIENCE, AND THE 'GUIDING HAND'

For the Victorines, the spiritual journey inevitably begins in a profound understanding of divine mystery and in an equally intentional effort at self-knowledge, the virtue from the time of Socrates to 'know thyself'. The journey, however, seldom 'ended'. Whether moving toward union with God through intellect or love, to identity with Christ in his full humanity, or soaring in flights of ecstatic spiritual 'inebriation', the pattern of the journey was always one of return to the world in selfless and compassionate love of neighbour. Given that trajectory, the spiritual life for the Victorines was dynamic, often in flux, intent on formation in virtue, and always driven by love of God *and* neighbour in the context of healthy integration of mind, body, world, and spirit.

Throughout the many forms and structures of the spiritual journey, the Victorines often had recourse to the use of the technical term 'guiding hand' or *manuductio* from *manu* or 'hand' and *ductio* or 'guide'.[19] By now we are not surprised to recognize that in the process of one's spiritual journey there could be many such 'guiding hands': Scripture, exegesis, symbols, prayer and contemplation, worship, love of neighbour. But one 'guiding hand' above all others served as teacher and master in the Victorine search for spiritual wisdom: experience – experience of God, of nature, of self, and of relationship in community. We can conclude our chapter on the spiritual journey by citing Richard of St Victor on the relative importance of text, teaching, and experience in the art of spiritual guidance. Richard says:

> Who is this Benjamin? Many know, some by knowledge, others by experience. Let those who know by teaching listen patiently; let those who have been taught by experience listen gladly. For a discourse concerning him – no matter how lengthy – can never satisfy anyone who has been able to know him even once by means of the teaching of experience (and I speak confidently).[20]

Richard of St Victor goes on to comment on the perennial questions in all spiritual traditions: How much from texts and teachers? How much from experience? Richard says:

> Certainly we learn many things concerning discretion by reading, many things by listening, and many things from innate judgement of our reason, yet we are never educated [literally 'led or guided out' from the same root, *ductio*] to the full concerning this without the teaching of experience.[21]

3. EXEGESIS:
LITERAL, SPIRITUAL, VISUAL

In meditation upon Scripture the Victorines seek two inter-related results: knowledge and virtue. Both knowledge and virtue, in turn, are grounded in love. Scripture is read by those who seek to live a life of compassion, that is, by those who love virtue. And Scripture is read by those who seek to know truth, that is, by those who love knowledge.

All philosophy and the arts are, for Hugh of St Victor and those who followed, of paramount importance for ascertaining truth and virtue in Scripture.[1] Such 'secular' studies are essential preliminaries to the understanding of both the literal and the spiritual senses of Scripture. Only when philosophy and the arts are firmly grasped can theology, tradition, experience, and the various ways of reading be employed to ascertain the letter, the sense, and the hidden meaning within a text. For the Victorines, reading was, on the one hand, 'reading' as we think of it today. But it was also much more. Victorine reading included, as well, the art and practice of prayer, meditation, and contemplation.

We can best grasp the meaning of Victorine reading by recognizing it as an ancient practice that is currently undergoing contemporary appropriation. Victorine reading is *lectio divina*. It is a conversation, a constant oscillation between study, listening, response, commitment, and virtue. There is also a certain, less tangible quality to *lectio divina* that might best be described as 'relational'. Basil Pennington, one of the wisest interpreters of the ancient practice of *lectio divina* for contemporary use, has said:

One of the most amazing statements in the Bible – and there are lots of amazing statements in the Bible – are those words of Jesus to us: "I no longer call you servants, but friends." This is almighty God speaking, the Lord of all creation. And God says it to you and to me: "Friend." Friend! What is more wonderful, more precious than a true friend, one who is there for us? One with whom we can share anything and everything, one with whom there is full communion and communication. Our communication with our Divine Friend needs to be a two-way street. And if we are smart, we let God get in the first word. This is precisely what *lectio divina* is: letting our Divine Friend speak to us through an inspired and inspiring Word. *Lectio* is meeting with a very special Friend who is God; listening to God, really listening; and responding, in intimate prayer and in the way we take that Word with us and let it shape our lives.[2]

Pennington goes on to extend the relational metaphor to include acquaintanceship, intimacy, and love. This is Hugh of St Victor's proposal as well: a programme of study and a method of reading to acquire knowledge and to live a life of virtue in relation to community, nature, and God.

HUGH OF ST VICTOR: FOUNDATIONS OF VICTORINE EXEGESIS

The history of biblical exegesis is both fascinating and frustrating: fascinating in its imaginative, intuitive, creative approach to reading Scripture, and frustrating in its varied use of common terms and methods. It is consistent in one respect, and that is the general consensus that there are at least two ways of reading Scripture: historically or literally and figuratively. Beyond this consensus is variety and disagreement enough for many, many books. The figurative reading is generally, though not always, thought to hold a key to the 'hidden' meaning of Scripture. Figurative readings are often referred to as 'spiritual' or 'mystical' approaches to Scripture. The spiritual senses are sometimes two, sometimes three. Often one spiritual sense is given the same name but burdened with different meanings. Some writers link the literal sense to one or more of the spiritual senses. Other schools hold to the essential unique importance of the literal sense alone.

Our task, however, is to examine Victorine exegesis, and for this purpose we will have to sketch an outline of their process in broad strokes. But as it is within the history of biblical interpretation in general, so also do various Victorines hold divergent points of view regarding methods of reading sacred texts. There is one consistent theme among all Victorines, however, and by now it should not surprise us: interrelatedness – in this case the interdependence of the senses of Scripture. As with the different elements within Victorine life that together comprised a single spiritual quest, so also do we find in the interrelation of senses in Victorine exegesis the forging of a comprehensive understanding of the art of reading.

By the medieval period, the four common ways in which Scripture was read included the literal/historical, allegorical, anagogical, and tropological senses. These are summarized in a well-known medieval couplet of unknown authorship:

> Lettera gesta docet, quid credas allegoria;
> Moralis quid agas, quo tendas anagogia.
> (The letter teaches what happened; the allegorical sense
> what to believe; the moral sense what to do, the
> anagogical sense where to direct our course.)[3]

The literal or historical sense refers to the events and realities of Jewish and early Christian history and deals with the significance of words in relation to things. Of the spiritual senses, the allegorical reveals the signification of things in relation to hidden deeds by which one can understand how persons and events can reveal the theological mysteries hidden within the text. Tropology consists of the signification of things in relation to hidden things to be done, that is, the application of the text to individual Christian practice. The anagogical sense points toward the path to God and eschatological fulfilment. Hugh speaks of anagogy as the uplifting of the soul through the visible things of the world into the invisible things of God and as 'the ascension or elevation of the mind to the heights of contemplation.'[4]

Though reading Scripture in these four ways is common in Hugh, he also often favours a threefold understanding of Scripture: one historical or literal sense and two spiritual senses, allegory and tropology. However, since various passages of Scripture do not always contain all three senses, Hugh cautions that we must not force upon the text a meaning that is not warranted:

> First of all, it ought to be known that Sacred Scripture has three ways of conveying meaning – namely, history, allegory, and tropology.[5] Divine utterances are placed in certain things which are intended to be understood spiritually only, certain things that emphasize the importance of moral conduct, and certain things said according to the simple sense of history . . . we do not try to find history everywhere, nor allegory everywhere, nor tropology everywhere.[6]

Unique to Hugh and the cause of some confusion in sorting out the work of the Victorines who followed him is what he calls his 'twofold fruit' of sacred reading. The fruit of sacred reading either (1) instructs the mind, or (2) instructs the reader in the moral life. Again, we encounter the relation of knowledge and virtue. On the basis of this 'twofold fruit', Hugh links the historical and allegorical reading with the instruction of the mind and the tropological reading with the moral life.[7] One confusion that results is that it becomes difficult to determine whether a Victorine exegete is primarily focused on the literal or the allegorical sense, since both are done with the intent of 'instructing the mind with knowledge'. Further complicating the issue is the relative function of love and knowledge in the interpretation of Scripture. Hugh says, for instance:

God dwells within the human heart in two ways, namely, through knowledge and through love. Yet, there is but one dwelling, for everyone who knows God loves God, and no one can love God who does not know God. Yet, knowledge and love of God differ in this way, namely, knowledge builds the house of faith while love, through virtue, paints the edifice as with color spread upon the whole.[8]

Here, history and allegory provide a kind of faith-knowledge, while tropology provides love and virtue. Hugh's insistence on the relation between the historical and allegorical sense is somewhat inexactly interpreted in Beryl Smalley's sharp distinction between Richard of St Victor, the strictly allegorical exegete, and Andrew of St Victor, the purely literal interpreter of Scripture. A more realistic appraisal is that both, as good and loyal disciples of Hugh, are pursuing readings that they believe 'build the house of faith' through knowledge rather than love. Further complicating the issue is Richard of St Victor's frequent habit of 'painting the house of faith' through love using the tropological sense.

Complete exegetical consistency is obviously not always the primary goal of Victorine writing. In utilizing the historical and spiritual interpretations of Scripture, Hugh is more interested in conforming to the Victorine habit of integration. In this case he integrates the foundational aspects of the history and narrative of Scripture with the anagogical ascent to God and the allegorical pursuit of doctrine. This synthesis is achieved primarily through the invocation of key biblical symbols rather than by means of logical discourse. The great scholar of the twelfth century, M.-D. Chenu once remarked, in relation to Hugh's definition of symbol, that the medieval period, throughout its culture, 'was an era of the symbol as much as, indeed more than, an era of dialectic.'[9]

VISUAL EXEGESIS AND SPIRITUAL EYES

Based upon their use of symbols and sacramental world view, the Victorines manage to transform traditional exegesis into 'visual' expressions of knowledge and virtue. Visual exegetical expressions become in turn effective objects of contemplation, illuminating spiritual pathways into God. The extent to which Victorine spirituality expresses itself visually is both unique and compelling. The practice has roots in the negative theology of Dionysius and in the concept of the spiritual senses found in Origen and Augustine and later in Bonaventure.

Basic to this 'visual' expression of Victorine spirituality is the definition of symbol and anagogy as the process of moving through the visible world into the invisible things of God. According to this tradition the natural world is, when observed in a contemplative way, a symbolic door into the 'invisible' world. In the same way, biblical images and symbols are themselves doors into the ineffable. It is but a small step, then, to move from literal, spiritual and figurative exegesis into visual exegesis in which the forms and images of Scripture are 'painted' as it were, in the mind and heart of the exegete/ contemplative. In the case of Hugh and Richard of St Victor, actual diagrams were composed that were to function as visual analogues of written exegesis. Whether the images were simply described in the text or actually diagrammed, they were intended to serve as a kind of 'internal icon' by means of which one might journey inward, encountering the internalized biblical symbol in an intensely personal way.

Visual exegesis is based on the concept of the 'spiritual eye'. In his commentary on the *Literal Sense of Genesis*, Augustine had suggested that there are three kinds of vision: corporeal, spiritual, and intellectual or mental. By the time of Hugh of St Victor, these ways of seeing had evolved into a metaphorical system of 'spiritual eyes' by which the soul utilized symbols and the teeming holiness of God's creation anagogically. In the *Didascalicon, On the Sacraments of the Christian Faith*, and the *Commentary* on the *Celestial Hierarchy* of Dionysius, Hugh speaks of a variety of 'spiritual eyes'. These include (1) the eye of the flesh or eye of nature which sees 'outside itself' (*extra se*) into that which is in the world; (2) the eye of reason or eye of the mind which sees 'inside itself' (*in se*) into the soul and that which is within the human spirit; and (3) the eye of contemplation which sees God in God's self and oneself in God (*intra se et supra se*). Each of these eyes function together as a whole: in moving ever closer to a vision of God, the previous 'vision' or way of seeing is never annihilated, but is rather integrated into the next. All of these 'eyes' need divine restoration, for all are inadequate by human capability alone. Hugh says that the eye of the flesh is restored by the practical arts of ethics and virtue; the eye of reason is restored by the theoretical arts; the eye of the mind is restored by contemplation or by the sacraments or through the created world; and the eye of contemplation is restored by faith.

Richard of St Victor, in his *Commentary on the Apocalypse of John*, speaks of four kinds of vision that correspond to the four senses of Scripture.[10] His four kinds of visions explain the diverse ways by which one might rise by means of symbols from sensible things to an understanding of the divine realities. The first two visions, Richard says, are 'corporal', the second two are 'spiritual'. The first two are described as vision by the 'eyes of flesh', the second two as by the 'eyes of the heart'.

Richard's first vision is correlated to the literal or historical sense. In this kind of vision we 'open the eye to exterior and visible things . . . yet since this vision is not sharp-sighted, it does not penetrate hidden things and therefore contains no mystical significance.' The second corporal vision by the eye of the flesh is correlated to the tropological sense when 'a form or action is revealed to our sense of exterior sight while interiorly a virtue of great mystical significance is contained.' Richard notes that the first vision is empty of mystery, while the second overflows with 'heavenly sacraments [or mysteries] through the work of virtue.'

The third vision, which is spiritual and seen through the

'eyes of the heart', is correlated to the allegorical sense of Scripture. This takes place when 'the soul is illuminated by the Holy Spirit by means of symbols of visible things and is led, through the imagination, by means of signs and figures to understand invisible things.' The fourth vision is correlated to the anagogical sense of Scripture and leads to contemplation. This fourth vision is initiated when 'the human spirit, by means of subtle and sweet internal aspirations and having touched nothing of mediating figures or visible things, is spiritually raised to contemplation of celestial things.' The third form of vision thus ascends by means of symbols to invisible things, while the fourth form of vision eschews the mediatory quality of symbols altogether, relying instead on unmediated revelation. Thus the third vision of hidden things is based on symbols, while the fourth vision 'is naked and pure and without the covering of any symbol or sign.' It is based purely on faith and is vision by means of contemplation.

In the *Mystical Ark*, Richard of St Victor incorporates and expands Hugh's use of the 'spiritual eyes' using them now, not in correlation with the senses of Scripture, but associating the various 'eyes' with levels of contemplation. Richard's use in the *Mystical Ark* can be outlined as follows:

First and Second Form of Contemplation:

Eye of the Flesh: Sees *visible* and *created* things in the imagination and according to reason, having as their object the form and image of visible and rational things.

Third Form of Contemplation

Eye of Reason: Sees *invisible* and *created* things in reason according to imagination, having as their object invisible things through their likeness to visible things.

Fourth Form of Contemplation

Eye of Understanding:

Sees *invisible* and *created* things in reason and according to reason having as their object the invisible spirit of celestial souls.

Fifth Form of Contemplation

Seeing by Means of Ecstasy of Mind:

Sees *invisible* and *uncreated* things, which are above but not contrary to reason having as their object the divine summit of simple unity.

Sixth Form of Contemplation

Eye of Faith:

Sees *invisible* and *uncreated* things that are above reason and are seemingly contrary to reason having as their object the Trinity of persons.

In this final form of contemplation Richard shifts Hugh's 'eye of contemplation' which had been restored or opened by faith to, simply, the 'eye of faith'.

VISUAL EXEGESIS AS SPIRITUAL PEDAGOGY

With the 'spiritual eyes' in place, it is a natural step to undertake biblical interpretation according to visual exegesis. In fact, Hugh of St Victor's *Mystical Ark of Noah* is an exploration in visual exegesis and spiritual pedagogy. The *Mystical Ark of Noah* describes an actual drawing of the ark of Noah. The drawing is no longer available to us, but, based on the description of the drawing, several scholars have reconstructed the basic contours of the drawing, as Hugh must have intended it.[11] In following Hugh's instructions, one is able to note the relation of word, text and image in visual exegesis, the influence of textual exegesis on visual exegesis, and the pedagogical application of the drawing of the ark of Noah to the spiritual disciplines of meditation and contemplation. For Hugh of St Victor, the ark reveals the soul to itself; the drawing seeks to restore a lost unity of heart and mind, and it restructures the soul in such a way that it becomes familiar to itself.

In the Ark of Noah treatises, Hugh of St Victor teaches the spiritual disciplines of *lectio, meditatio,* and *contemplatio* that are to be practised through the text and the drawing. The drawings affirm the pedagogical value of images and serve a 'mystical' function that is similar to that of Orthodox icons. For Hugh and the Victorines, these drawings 'speak' because, as with writing, they are a 'word' from God. The two modes of exegesis, of course, give expression to two different kinds of writing: alphabetic and iconographic. The pedagogical function of pictorial or iconographic writing is not a degraded substitute for the alphabetic. Hugh says, in fact, in a third treatise on the ark, *The World's Vanity,* that the words of humanity are many because the heart of humanity is not one. He adds that, unlike the multiplicity of spoken or written discourse, a drawing provides a kind of totality that our spoken, fragmenting words cannot. A drawing, in other words, reveals unity.

The drawing, then, becomes the exterior corollary of the route to interior reunification. It is significant that Hugh should claim that it is the 'heart' of humanity that is not one, for in the work of restoration it is, finally, the heart that directs the soul in contemplation from division to unification.

The drawings of Hugh are also analogous to the triple senses of Scripture. They can, for instance, be linked to the anagogical function of symbols. The drawings function, as Hugh describes the function of symbols, as 'a collection of visible forms to demonstrate the properties of invisible things.' The drawing of the ark of Noah also serves this anagogical function in that it is *manuductio* (a guiding hand) for the contemplation of invisible things. The drawing thus allows the exegete to move contemplatively through symbolic images derived from Scripture into the holy, into divine reality.

Through Hugh of St Victor's visual application of reading, meditation, and contemplation one encounters a pedagogy based on unity. Through the exercises, the divine image or spark that grounds the very centre of the human soul is acknowledged allegorically, lived tropologically, and entered anagogically. And, in the best Victorine fashion, the drawing of the ark of Noah exists as a kind of internal icon of divine inner dwelling through which wisdom (*sapientia*) is restored by contemplative knowledge and the good (*bonitas*) is restored through contemplative love.

TEMPLES OF THE SOUL

In many religious traditions temples, churches, cities, castles, arks, and edifices of many kinds are allegorical figures used to describe the spiritual edifice of men and women: they are equated with the soul. As with models of the spiritual journey, edifices map the journey of the soul into God. They can also be utilized as tools to teach devotional practices and as steps in the process of constructing a life of contemplation and action. The Victorine use of such symbols demonstrates their interest in the material things of creation as material images and theophanies. Contemplative practices are based on symbolic structures such as houses, temples, and arks that are utilized as avenues of access to the divine, invisible realm. 'Symbols', as Bernard McGinn has noted, are 'expressions of mystical anagogy, which bring order and clarity to rich symbolic presentations of the ineffable mystery of the divine-human encounter.'[12] As allegories of the soul these symbolic structures present a special marriage between logic and biblical images that result in compelling examples of visual exegesis. This vivid form of exegesis fostered the dynamic process initiated by Augustine and Gregory the Great: introversion and ascension wherein one moves inward to the soul in order to ascend upward toward God. A sampling of Victorine 'temples of the soul' will help us to see this blending of exegesis, contemplation, the spiritual journey, and entry, in a spatial or architectural sense, into God.

RICHARD OF ST VICTOR: THE TABERNACLE OF THE LORD IS THE SOUL

Below is a portion of a simple and straightforward sermon by Richard of St Victor. It is of interest because it states explicitly that the tabernacle or church is symbolically equivalent to the soul. Richard uses the construction of the church within the soul as an allegory of the active and contemplative life. Each element of the church is considered in detail. The walls of the church, for instance, represent the contemplative life, as we might expect, in that they are raised from the foundation, which is Christ, vertically toward heaven. The roof represents acts of compassion which spread out horizontally to reach out in love to one's neighbour.

In a later work, the *Mystical Ark*, Richard gives a much more elaborate allegorical and tropological reading of an edifice. But both works bear the essential mark of Victorine spiritual exegesis: the church, the ark, and the tabernacle are to be 'built' within the human soul so God may dwell therein. After describing each element of the church in detail, Richard summarizes:

> Your tabernacle, Lord, is made holy. The *tabernacle of the Lord according to the tropological sense is the soul* . . . Therefore, *the church itself is the soul*; the sides are virtues, the mortar is love [which binds all together], the foundation is Christ, the walls are contemplation, the roof is compassion, the length is faith, the height is hope, the width is love, the sacrarium represents those things which are made in the image of God, the choir represents those things made in the likeness of God, the nave is the way of the senses, the atrium the way of flesh, the altar is the contrite heart. It has clear windows indicating spiritual senses, a tower indicating the name of the Lord, symbols

indicating preaching, interior plaster indicating the cleanliness of the heart, exterior plaster indicating the cleanliness of the body, twelve candles for the teaching of the twelve Apostles. Its Bishop is the holy Trinity. Therefore, make a great effort, dear friends, every one of you, make a great effort so that, according to what has been said above, *the tabernacle of God might come to be made within you so that there God might deign to dwell.* It is indeed a great thing to have the honor, worthiness, sublimity, security, and glory of God dwell within you. And so it is certainly being provided to us that we are so made inwardly and outwardly, inwardly by faith, outwardly by compassion, so that the Lord of Majesty comes to us and we are found worthy to have divine mansions made within us. Yet since we are not able to be such things without God's grace, we ask incessantly for this necessary thing. And for just such works, grace will be given, and not only grace, but glory also.[13]

THE CHURCH THAT ACHARD BUILDS: CHRIST AND GOD WITHIN

In *Sermon 13*: 'Sermon for the Dedication of a Church', Achard of St Victor uses the images of house, church and temple to take us deep into his Trinitarian and incarnational theology. The images also are used to comment on the nature of contemplation, and a visual exegesis of 1 Corinthians 1:24, that Christ, anointed with the Spirit, is 'the power and wisdom of God'. Through the medium of visual exegesis, the sermon allows Achard to articulate one of the key ideas of Victorine spirituality: that the Christian is Christ's dwelling place.

Achard begins the central part of his discourse on the dwelling of Christ and God as Trinity in the soul as an interpretation of Solomon's temple from 1 Kings 5–6. The temple is built from hewn stone, cedar wood, and gold. Achard uses these three materials to build 'three houses' of which he says, 'all three of these houses are built in one heart, they are there joined into one house, so that in some sense they are both three and one. Three in one and one in three, one threefold house, as one might expect of the house of the one, triune God.'[14] The Son is especially described as the builder of the house of God, but he does not build it for himself alone, but for the Trinity together; it is a single house in three. The 'houses' are built successively within one another with a door leading from one 'house' to the next. Seven columns support each 'house'. The construction in the soul of the temple and of the three houses of the single temple can be outlined as follows:

Achard's Temple of the Soul

Unity of Solomon's Temple:
>   Hewn Stone
>   Cedar Wood
>   Finest Gold

Trinity of Houses:

	Father	*Holy Spirit*	*Son*
Material:	Hewn Stone	Cedar Wood	Finest Gold
Quality of House:	House of Power	House of Anointing	House of Wisdom
Nature of House:	Love	Delight	Contemplation
Location in Temple:	Exterior House	Interior House	Inmost House
Columns:	7 of Virtue	7 of Joy	7 of Contemplation
Aspects of Christ:	The Way	The Life	The Truth
Nature of Christ:	Flesh of Christ	Spirit of Christ	Divinity of Christ

Seven Columns

Seven Stone Columns of Exterior Virtue:
>   Obedience
>   Providence
>   Congratulation
>   Compassion
>   Imitation of Christ
>   Exhortation of Neighbour
>   Divine Love

Seven Cedar Columns of Interior Joy and Spiritual Delight:
    Purity
    Condition of Righteousness
    Possession of Beatitude
    Taste of Divine Sweetness
    Fullness of Divine Sweetness
    Appearance and Form of Righteousness
    Beauty of Spiritual Purity

Seven Golden Columns of Inmost Contemplation of Highest Good:
    Participation in Physical Things
    Participation in Spiritual Creation: Creation
    Participation in Spiritual Creation: Justification
    Participation in Spiritual Creation: Beatification
    Participation in the Eternal Plan of All Things
    Participation in Predestination of the Saints
    Participation in the Unity and Trinity of the Godhead

Particularly intriguing is Achard of St Victor's insistence on *integrating body, mind, and spirit.* Patristic and medieval Christianity is often criticized for a dualistic division between body and spirit. Contemporary Christians rightly insist on a total spirituality of body, mind and spirit. But we must not judge the tradition too harshly as Achard so well illustrates. He says:

> As the one person of Christ subsists in three essences, that is, of the flesh, the spirit, and divinity . . . When these three houses are built in us, we too become wholly the house of God. Our body becomes the house of God on account of the first house; our spirit, on account of the second; our mind, on account of the third. God is glorified and carried by us in our body, and there God dwells as if bodily; God dwells spiritually in our spirit, and intellectually in our mind.[15]

The Victorines were especially fascinated by the spiritual significance of numbers,[16] and Achard was no exception. In this sermon, numerous 'hewn stones' are detailed according to the number four, or quaternary which is associated with fullness or completeness. A few of these four-cornered 'hewn stones'

from which the walls of virtue were to be constructed are as
follows. Note that Achard's rich imagination finds more than
one composition for stones of heaven and of Christ:

A Stone of the Heavenly Square:

Matthew

Mark

Luke

John

A Stone of the Heavenly Square:

Christ's Divinity

Christ's Humanity

Angels

Humanity

A Stone of the Heavenly Square:

Wisdom

Understanding

Redemption

Sanctification

A Stone of the Goodness of Christ:

Temperance

Prudence

Righteousness

Fortitude

A Stone of the Goodness of Christ:

Poverty

Thirst for God

Weeping

Bearing Persecution

Stone of Love of Neighbour and of God:

Of Neighbour: Gentle of Heart

Of God: Humility of Heart

Of Neighbour: Lightening Burden

Of God: Easy Yoke of Christ

Stone of Loving Neighbour as Oneself:

With Whole Heart

With Whole Mind

With Whole Soul

With Whole Strength

Stone of Explicit Love of Neighbour:

Correct the Restless

Encourage the Fainthearted

Support the Weak

Kindness to All

Stone of the Love of God (Firmly Attaches Our Spiritual House to Christ):

Love God with Fervent Hearts

Love God with Upright Minds

Love God with Abundant Strength

Love God with the Life of Our Soul

Stone of Divine Sovereignty:

God's Love of Measureless Breadth

God's Love of Eternal Length

God's Love of the Height of Power

God's Love of the Very Depth of Wisdom

Achard ends his sermon on the construction of the house of God within the soul in what is perhaps the only way that can do justice to the wisdom and charity of God: with a song of praise:

> O house to be contemplated! O house one and three, built in its entirety upon a single rock! O you who dwell in a mud house, you who have built your house upon sand, where you waver and grow bitter and dark, look here and gaze upon a solid house, a joyful house, a luminous house! Look and long, admire and aspire, consider and desire, desire and hasten, hasten and enter, enter and occupy. Occupy and love, occupy and delight, occupy and contemplate.[17]

HUGH OF ST VICTOR: VISUAL EXEGESIS AS MANDALA

Hugh of St Victor invites the reader to enter the heart's secret place and 'make a dwelling place for God, make a temple, make a home, make a tabernacle, make an ark of the covenant, make an ark of the flood, for whatever name you use, the Lord's house within is one.'[18] Hugh guides us into this 'Lord's house within' by means of his drawing the ark. In reconstructing the drawing, Grover Zinn has described the ark as a Christian mandala.[19] In it the ark becomes a symbol of the cosmos in which the spiritual quest takes place in the context of sacred history. As such, this form of visual exegesis employs biblical symbols as primary bearers of meaning and as agents of transformation. The opening description of this visual image begins:

> The figure of this spiritual building that I am going to present to you is Noah's ark. Your eye shall see outwardly, so that your soul may be fashioned to its likeness inwardly. You will see there certain colors, shapes, and figures which will be pleasant to behold. But you must understand that these are put there, that from them you may learn wisdom,

instruction, and virtue to adorn your soul ... I have painted the whole person of Christ, head and members, in a visible form, so that when you view the whole you can understand more easily what will be said about each part. I want to represent that person to you as Isaiah testifies he saw him ... "I saw the Lord sitting on a throne high and exalted." (Is. 6:1).[20]

In the drawing, various iconographic devices depict the interior stages of the spiritual life as the soul advances toward perfection. The ark is drawn with Christ's body, his head, hands and feet extending beyond the ark. The drawing portrays the Christ figure as the Lord of history embracing the created circle of the cosmos in his arms. The mandalic quality of the drawing is heightened in this vision of Christ encircling the cosmos: it implies that to ascend to God one must enter into the interior depths of the self. Twelve ladders, each a series of three ladders representing major stages in the contemplative life, represent degrees of ascent.[21] The stages were listed earlier in Chapter Two on the spiritual journey.

Just as the visible world was meant to instruct humanity concerning the invisible things of creation, so the visible symbol of the ark drawing is meant to conduct the mind's eye to the apprehension of a higher reality.

RICHARD OF ST VICTOR: THE ARK AS INTERNAL ICON

We will end our survey of Victorine temples of the soul with a brief look at Richard of St Victor's *Mystical Ark*. Further exploration of this treatise will appear in Chapter Six on contemplation.

With Richard's *Mystical Ark* we once again find Victorine exegesis moving into the realm of the visual. In biblical images of edifices Victorine spirituality recognized symbols that functioned anagogically by illustrating the process of ascent to God as initiated by an inward movement into the realm of the soul.

Richard of St Victor, better than any other of the Victorine masters, was able to manipulate visual imagery in the service of contemplative ascent. With the Ark of the Covenant mounted by the golden cherubim as described in Exodus 25, Richard was able to envision both movements into the soul and ascent to God in a single image. The ark itself represents the created world as well as the soul and functions as a symbol of contemplative movement inward. The cherubim, as angelic creatures of the celestial realm, proved a ready symbol of contemplative movement upward into God. Since the cherubim are fastened to the ark, the over-arching symbol of the contemplative process was one of intimate connection between God, the human soul, and the created world. Contemplative ascent was symbolically grounded in the world and in the soul.

Richard's visual image, as with Hugh's ark of Noah, is mandalic. Forming a womb-like circle atop the ark, the wings of the cherubim encircle the space where, according to Richard, Christ is continually born within the centre/soul of the human person. The complete vision contemplated and lived according to Richard's spiritual teaching is intended as an interior icon. Through the interior icon, an image is carried continually in the heart and mind of the contemplative. The icon within is available, in whatever we do or wherever we are, to remind us and assure us of God's continual presence.

As with Hugh's ark of Noah, Richard of St Victor based his moral and spiritual teaching on the literal materials from Genesis 25. From these materials he constructs an interior edifice for the human heart:

Six Kinds of Contemplation in the *Mystical Ark* [22]

	First	Second	Third	Fourth	Fifth	Sixth
Symbol:	Wood	Gilding	Crown	Mercy Seat	1st Cherubim	2nd Cherubim
Entry Point:	Natural World................			Soul	Transcendent.................	
Creator/ Creature:	Visible & Created		Invisible & Created		Invisible & Uncreated	
Works/ Grace:	Human Effort.................			Effort & Grace	Grace Alone	
Grade:	Imagination......		Reason.........		Above Reason	Beyond Reason
Object:	Visible Things		Invisible Through Visible Things	Invisible Things Of Ourselves	Unity	Trinity
Eyes:	Eye of Flesh		Eye of Reason	Eye of Understanding	Seeing in Ecstasy of Mind	Eye of Faith

With Richard of St Victor pre-eminently, we see in Victorine spirituality the inseparable union of its parts. As Victorine exegesis moves toward a visual form, its symbols take on a multi-valiant quality. They function not only as visual representations of biblical narratives, but also as signposts on the spiritual journey, as markers of anagogic ascent into God, as guides to personal appropriation of doctrinal theology, as images of mystical union, as grades of contemplative consciousness, and as models of compassion.

4. THE PATHS OF KNOWLEDGE AND LOVE

What is the relation between the path of knowledge and the path of love in the contemplative ascent to God? In the famous vision shared by Augustine and his mother at Ostia recorded in the *Confessions*, we can see an early example of the difficulty of 'sorting out' these two paths. One can sense the struggle Augustine undergoes as he tries to put his experience of the 'vision of God' into words. Words and phrases (placed in italics) that evoke this relation between love and knowledge seem both to compliment and contradict one another as he strains to describe the vision:

> As the *flame of love burned* stronger in us and raised us higher towards the eternal God, our *thoughts* ranged over the whole compass of material things in their various degrees, up to the heavens themselves, from which the sun and the moon and the stars shine down upon the earth. Higher still we climbed, *thinking and speaking* all the while in *wonder* at all that you have made. At length we came to our own souls and passed beyond them to that place of everlasting plenty, where you feed Israel for ever with the food of *truth*. There life is that *Wisdom* by which all these things that we *know* are made, all things that were, have been and all that are yet to be. But that *Wisdom* is not made. It is as it has always been and as it will be forever or, rather, I should not say that it has been or will be, for it simply is, because eternity is not in the past or in the future. And while we *spoke* of the eternal *Wisdom*, *longing* for and *straining* for it with all the

> strength of our *hearts*, for one fleeting instant we reached
> out and touched it. Then with a sigh, leaving our spiritual
> harvest bound to it, we returned to the sound of our own
> *speech*, in which each *word* has a beginning and ending,
> far different from your Word, our Lord, who abides in
> himself for ever, yet never grows old and gives new life to
> all things.[1]

What 'touches' God, the mind or the heart? For Augustine, the
answer is not clear. The broad family of words relating to
the mind (thoughts, thinking, truth, speaking, speech, and
word), and the broad family of words signifying heart (love,
burned, wonder, longing, straining, hearts) seem to compete
for the best expression of the soul's thirst for contact with God.
Or do they work together? And what are we to do with
'Wisdom'? Is Wisdom grounded in love, or forged and tempered
in the mind?

Hugh of St Victor opens his *Didascalicon* with the words,
'Of all things to be sought, the first is that Wisdom in which
the Form of the Perfect Good stands fixed. Wisdom illuminates
humanity so that humanity may *know* itself.' Here Hugh
appears to equate Wisdom with knowledge, the way of the
mind. Later, in the same paragraph, he associates Wisdom
with the mind through education. He even uses the occasion
to quote the famous Oracle of Apollo: γνωθι σεαυτον, '*know*
thyself'. Self-knowledge, as we have seen, is a key initial step
toward God in all Victorine spirituality. Yet in another work,
his commentary on Dionysius the Areopagite's *Celestial Hierarchy*, Hugh equates knowledge (*scientia*) with the realm of
the philosophers and Wisdom (*sapientia*) as the scandalous
'knowledge' of the Christian, which is at its core the '*love* of
Christ crucified'. 'Wisdom' itself is ambiguous. Is it knowledge?
Is it a special form of love?

These questions may not have answers. Or perhaps, in
looking closely at Victorine spirituality, we might more prop-
erly say that the answers are many. The Victorines, in a way
typical of medieval mysticism and spirituality, had an intense

concern for analysis of the affective and intellective powers of the soul and the manner in which these take part in the soul's ascent to God. Love and knowledge, for the Victorines, are the two fundamental powers of the soul. As their contemporary, Isaac of Stella, wrote in his *Letter on the Soul*, love and knowledge are 'the two feet by which the soul journeys into God.'

One example of ordered love and charity in Victorine writing is Richard of St Victor's depiction of the children of Jacob as allegories of various levels of self-understanding, virtue, knowledge, and love. Another of Richard's examples explores the role of desire and love in the contemplative ascent into inner-Trinitarian subjectivity, personhood, and love. Knowledge, likewise, is ordered to include a variety of meanings. These include reason, thinking, understanding, meditation, contemplation, and wisdom. Hugh of St Victor writes, concerning knowledge, of the importance of integrating ancient philosophy and Christian theology in ways that echo today's contextual theology.

The relative value of the paths of knowledge and the paths of love are always in the forefront of Victorine teaching on union with God. An excellent example of this relation is Thomas Gallus' use of the angelic hierarchy to describe a comprehensive spiritual path to God. Within this hierarchy the individual paths of knowledge and love are represented respectively by the cherubim and the seraphim. More often than not, the seraphim, or love, circle nearest to God. Yet at the same time the Victorines also recognized and emphasized the order of love and the order of knowledge as mutually enhancing. But even if love seems to be the highest transformative power available to the human soul, it is not a power that is in any way anti-intellectual. Victorines would have been in full agreement with the famous phrase of Gregory the Great, that 'love is itself [a form] of understanding.'[2] As we shall see, however, Victorine spirituality has finally more do with simplicity, humility, and compassion, than with critical analysis.

Taken as a whole, the Victorines found many ways to express

this mutually affecting relationship. As we might expect, the various expressions of the relationship between love and knowledge by the Victorines affected their exegesis, their teaching on the process of the spiritual quest, their practice of contemplation, and the manner in which they described deification and mystical union. In this they are no different than Augustine at Ostia. Augustine's description of the process of union with God illustrates something of the dilemma of the contemplative ascent: it is, finally, a kind of oscillation between compassionate love and contemplative knowledge.

LOVE AND KNOWLEDGE AS SPIRITUAL CATEGORIES

One ought to be sensitive to the wide variety of terminology medieval spiritual writers use to describe love and knowledge. We saw something of this variety in the quote above from Augustine's *Confessions*. Remembering that not all of these categories are strictly categories of mind or heart alone, we can name a few of the more common as follows:

Love		Knowledge
Love		**Knowledge**
Affect		Intellect
Heart		Mind
Love as:	*Amor*	Thought
	Caritas	Reason
	Pietas	Intellect
	Dilectio	Intelligence
Feelings/Sensations		Understanding
Desire		Knowledge
Wonder		Wonder
Wisdom		Wisdom

Adding to a potential for misunderstanding is the Latin word *mens*. This word is often translated as 'mind', but in many ways the Latin conception of *mens* comes closer to our contemporary conception of 'soul'. This is because the Latin *mens* as 'mind' was painted from a much broader anthropological palate in Victorine times than in our own. The anthropological trichotomy usually used to describe the medieval conception of *mens*: *sensus-ratio-intelligentia* (sense, reason, understanding) is even richer in Victorine writing. With the Victorines *mens* is often expanded to include *sensus-imaginatio-ratio-intellectus-intelligentia* (sense, imagination, reason, intellect, understanding). As readers of Victorine spirituality we must be on guard not to limit the Victorine category of mind to our own narrow understanding of 'reason'.

Three other important insights with regard to the categories of love and intellect, which we will explore in more detail below, ought to be mentioned. The first insight is the category of 'obtaining knowledge through unknowing', which the Victorines inherit from Dionysius the Areopagite. This form of 'dark knowledge' or apophatic knowing, in acknowledging God's radical transcendence beyond human categories of understanding, employs the methodology of negation in its ascent to God. More will be said concerning this 'dark way' in Chapter Five. The second insight, related to the first, is the Victorine use of categories of mind to indicate knowledge that is 'beyond' or 'above' mind, a transcendence of mind. These categories include, for instance, ecstasy of the mind (*excessus mentis*) and alienation of the mind (*alienatio mentis*). The third important insight is charity or compassion. Compassion in Victorine spirituality is that form of Christian love that expresses love of God through love of neighbour and which brings a complimentary balance to contemplation.

HUMAN ANTHROPOLOGY AND DIVINE ATTRIBUTES

When we speak of love and knowledge we speak at one and the same time of human anthropology and of divine attributes. Humans have capacities to love and to think. God *is* knowledge. And God *is* love. Though the correspondence is not equal

– humanity and God are not identical – Victorine spirituality is clear: in very important respects humanity and God 'share' certain attributes. Repentence (*metanoia*) is a change in the human heart and mind that turns us to the heart and mind of God. Thus, to know *something* of divine love we can look to human love as a reflection of divine love. Richard of St Victor is particularly adept at illustrating how humanity and God share the quality of love, particularly love as 'charity'.

Richard's preoccupation with love is a reflection of the time in which he lived. One recent scholar describes the twelfth century's extraordinary interest in love by saying:

> In the course of the centuries, thanks to the moral preaching of pastors, thanks to the work of doctors and theologians, an immense force of reflection was brought to bear on love, the last word of the Christian message. But it can be said that never did more men and women speak of love and speak of it better than in the twelfth century.[3]

By the beginning of the twelfth century, troubadours from southern France created a new poetic vision of love. The troubadours not only initiated a major literary movement of the medieval period, but with their concepts of romantic love, they profoundly influenced Western culture. At the same time that these travelling poets were giving expression to romantic love, the religious writers of the era were exploring Christian charity and mystical love. The twelfth century abounded in religious works on love. There were numerous commentaries on the Song of Songs (Richard of St Victor himself wrote such a commentary), as well as other works and genres dealing with the subject of love. The Cistercians Bernard of Clairvaux, Aelred of Rievaux, and William of St Thierry were known especially for their writings on mystical love and human friendship.

For Richard, as for the twelfth century in general and Victorine spirituality in particular, the highest form of love is charity or what we would refer to as compassion. Richard says of charity:

> Let each person examine their consciousness; without
> doubt and without contradiction they will discover that
> just as nothing is better than charity, so nothing is more
> pleasing than charity. Nature herself teaches us this;
> many experiences do the very same.[4]

The power of charity, *caritas*, is that it implies another person
to which it is directed. It was in exploring the implications of
this fact that Richard of St Victor made his important contributions concerning the nature of the relation of human to
divine love. The key to this relation is the *imago Dei*, the
image or likeness of God within the human person. God is by
definition perfect charity, or outpouring of generous love, and
as such requires someone equal to God toward whom to direct
this love: 'And in those who are mutually loved . . . the perfection of each, in order to be completed, requires with equal
reason a sharer of the love that has been shown to them.'[5]
Richard works out his new notion of the person primarily in
terms of the Trinity, but as the divine mystery and the human
mystery are always in some sense connected, the definition
can be used analogously to apply to the human person as well.
A contemporary scholar sums up the relation between human
and divine love based on charity by saying:

> The human person, then, like the divine person, is called
> to share love: this is what makes it what it is truly
> meant to be. Being made in the image and likeness of God
> means being made to share in the shared love of the
> Trinity, and like the Trinity, to communicate that love to
> others.[6]

Richard of St Victor makes this especially clear in his *Four
Degrees of Violent Charity*. The third degree of charity involves
the 'death' of the soul into God. But at the fourth and higher
stage, a new creature rises with Christ to live a life of loving
service to others, i.e., a life of charity. Thus charity is equated
with imitation of Christ and the life of virtue.

We will now look in more detail at a few of the Victorines

as they trace the path of love and path of understanding. It is along these paths that humanity is guided inward to the self, outward in charity toward our neighbours and the world, and along contemplative routes into God.

RICHARD OF ST VICTOR AND THE FULLNESS OF KNOWLEDGE

Richard of St Victor is interested not only in the path of love, but also in the way of knowledge. Various scholars have concluded that Richard is able to 'synthesize' affect and reason and that in his writings love and knowledge mutually assist in the assent into God.[7]

We have already looked at Richard of St Victor's *Twelve Patriarchs* in the chapter on the spiritual journey (see pp. 49–52). There we encountered Richard's allegory of the twelve sons of Jacob. The birth of the final son, Benjamin, represents the birth of contemplation and the inception of the consciousness of divine presence. But this birth comes at a price: the death of Rachel who represents 'reason'. Richard says that Benjamin represents two kinds of contemplation, both of which are defined in the context of the death of Rachel, the death of reason:

> Nevertheless we are able fittingly to understand different kinds of contemplation by the death of Rachel and the ecstasy of Benjamin since it is agreed that there are two kinds of contemplation above reason and both pertain to Benjamin. Indeed, the first is above reason, but not beyond reason; however, the second is both above and beyond reason. Surely those things are above reason, but not beyond reason which cannot be investigated or refuted by reason, although *reason experiences their existence*. Now we call those things both above and beyond reason, the existence of which *seems to contradict all human reason*. They are such things as what we believe concerning the unity of the Trinity and many things concerning the body

of Christ that we hold on the indubitable authority of faith.[8]

Thus there are those things 'above and beyond' reason, accessible only through faith.

On the other hand, in our chapter above on exegesis, we looked briefly at Richard of St Victor's *Mystical Ark* (see pp. 74–5). In that treatise, Richard focuses on Exodus 25, which is one of the pre-eminent texts on the promise of the presence of God. The passage occurs in the context of God's instruction to Moses concerning the construction of the Ark of the Covenant and the two cherubim that are attached to it. Moses is told to, 'Make one cherub at one end, and one cherub at the other; of one piece with the mercy-seat you shall make the cherubim at its two ends. The cherubim shall spread out their wings above, overshadowing the mercy-seat with their wings. They shall face each other; the faces of the cherubim shall be turned towards the mercy-seat' (vv. 19–20). Then, in verse 22, Moses is made a promise by God: 'There I will meet you, and from above the mercy-seat, from between the two cherubim that are on the ark of the covenant, I will deliver to you all my commands for the Israelites.' In other words, God promises Moses that upon the mercy seat, between the two cherubim, God will meet with and speak with Moses and the people of Israel. God promises in these verses, in other words, to be ever present and ever available upon the ark.

In Hebrew, 'cherubim' means 'fullness of knowledge'. From the time of the Jewish exegete, Philo of Alexandria, through the Greek Patristic writers and on into the Latin tradition of the West from the time of Augustine, the cherubim came to be understood as a symbol of perfection in wisdom and fullness of knowledge.[9] The mercy seat itself came to be associated with the incarnation of Christ. By the time of the Victorines, the promise of divine presence was a promise to be fulfilled in the shadow of the wings of the cherubim, that is, in the shadow of the fullness or perfection of knowledge. Richard of St Victor says, in speaking of the final levels of contemplation where the soul is given the grace to 'see' God, that 'Perhaps not without cause did this last material product and angelic figure receive the name "cherubim"; perhaps for the reason that without the addition of this highest grace no one would be able to attain to fullness of knowledge.'[10]

In the *Mystical Ark*, which is subtitled 'The Grace of Contemplation', the promise of the presence of God is manifested in its highest form under the wings and in the shadow of the contemplative's attainment of the 'fullness of knowledge'. And when we recall that for the Victorines exegetical interpretations of biblical texts having to do with edifices or buildings include the 'construction' of that edifice in the very soul of the Christian, we see that the internalized promise of divine presence is also accomplished in this 'fullness of knowledge'.

How then, does the 'death of reason' (Rachel) at the birth of contemplation (Benjamin) coincide with the highest level of contemplation as the 'fullness of knowledge' (cherubim)? The answer is based in part on the Victorine distinction between the spiritual practices of thinking, meditation, and contemplation.[11] Though they are distinct, they all fall under the category of 'intellect' not love. 'Full knowledge' for the Victorines includes all three components. And though contemplation, as we will see more fully in the following chapter, does move 'above and beyond' reason, it is none the less described in categories of reason and intellect. 'Reason' is the human faculty in relation to which contemplation is explained, even as contemplation itself exceeds reason.

To distinguish thinking, meditation, and contemplation, Richard notes that:

> It ought to be known that we regard one and the same object in one way by means of thinking, we examine it in another way by means of meditation and we marvel at it in another way by means of contemplation ... concerning one and the same object, thinking proceeds in one way, meditation in another, and contemplation in quite a different way.[12]

Thus it is not the object – be it nature or the soul or God – that changes as it is being observed, but rather the way in which we understand the object itself that alters. Richard has a charming and insightful way of illustrating these three modes of 'knowledge' by comparing them to various patterns of birds in flight:

> Certainly if we consider this rightly, we see the form of this thing daily in the birds of the sky. Now you may see some raising themselves up on high; now others plunging themselves into lower regions and often repeating the same manner of their ascent and descent. You may see some turning to the side, now to the right, now to the left, and while coming down a little ahead now in this part, now in that, or advancing themselves almost not at all, repeating many times with great constancy the same changes of their movements [thinking] . . . You may see how others turn themselves in a circle, and how suddenly and how often they repeat the same or a similar path – one time a little wider, another time slightly smaller, but always returning to the same place [meditation]. One may see others suspending themselves in one and the same place for a long time with trembling and often rapidly vibrating wings and, through motion, maintain themselves motionless by their agitation [contemplation].[13]

It is this last form of knowledge – contemplation – that, for Richard, allows the fullest and most pure process of 'clinging in wonder to manifestations of divine wisdom'.

For Hugh of St Victor *lectio* (reading and thinking), meditation and contemplation are also spiritual practices that draw the soul into union with God. As with Richard 'fullness of knowledge' in Hugh is a comprehensive discipline involving at one and the same time mapping the spiritual journey, setting out a practice of prayer, illuminating Scripture, defining doctrinal categories and cultivating spiritual understanding. The interrelation of these disciplines in Hugh can be outlined according to the following table:

States of Spiritual Life	Spiritual Practice	Meaning of Scripture	Law/Grace	Eye
Beginning	Reading	Literal	Natural Law	Eye of Flesh
Progressing	Meditation	Allegorical	Law of Scripture	Eye of Reason
Perfected	Contemplation	Tropological	Grace	Eye of Contemplation

Richard of St Victor, however, is not satisfied with the flexibility of categories of mind, even when stretched to include the highest forms of contemplation. He ends the *Mystical Ark* by defining three 'modes of contemplation' that correspond to ecstatic visions or understanding 'above' and 'beyond' mind. These include (1) *dilatio mentis*, or expansion and broadening of the mind; (2) *sublevatio mentis*, or raising up of the mind; and (3) *alienatio mentis/escessus mentis*, or alienation of mind/ecstasy of mind. All these 'modes of contemplation', though defined in relation to mind, are without a doubt above and beyond mind. They are certainly intended, as Richard says, to take us into 'the secret places of divine incomprehensibility'. As such they reflect an essential divine reality: the transcendent fullness of the mystery of God is beyond reason, beyond knowledge, and finally incomprehensible.

THOMAS GALLUS AND THE BURNING LOVE OF THE SERAPHIM

Representing some of the finest articulations of the integration of rational and affective strands of mysticism found in the Christian spiritual tradition, it is appropriate that Thomas Gallus is receiving renewed attention. Gallus' integrative sensibility is inherited from a number of medieval and pre-Christian sources.[14] The *Prologue* to his third *Commentary on the Song of Songs* serves as a primary example of his ability to weave these strands together into a cohesive whole.

As Richard of St Victor used the cherubim as an anagogic symbol of the 'fullness of knowledge', Thomas Gallus, as was outlined in Chapter Two, uses the complete angelic hierarchy as a comprehensive map of the spiritual journey. But whereas the cherubim signify the path of the intellect, the seraphim, by tradition stretching back to the time of Dionysius the Areopagite, signify the path of love. Though Gallus' *Prologue* is a sustained exploration of the relation between intellect and love, it is the seraphim who circle in the 'most immediate proximity' to God. Thus, ultimately for Gallus, love is the supreme path to God. But the route of love does not exclude the mind. On that point Gallus is clear: both the cherubim (mind) and the seraphim (love) are necessary components of the soul's quest for God. Knowledge and love as exemplified by the 'angels of the soul' represent variations in the nature, medium, and manner of God's presence to us. For Gallus, each angelic path into mystical consciousness is also a path that reflects relative proximity to God, a theophany within which God's essence is clothed for our 'reception'.

In the *Prologue* Thomas Gallus uses the simple metaphor of a 'kiss' to summarize the profound complexities of language, love, and mystical union. For Gallus, the kiss is a metaphor of language and of language silenced; the lips that must be silent in a kiss are the same lips that speak of longing and of wisdom. Yet in Gallus' metaphor the silence of the kiss, which represents the death of the intellect and the ineffable secession of speech, is also the birth of passion and charity. The kiss is a metaphor of love; the same lips that speak in silence spark passion.

This kiss, and Thomas Gallus' *Prologue* in general, function as an outline of his mature theology and spirituality. The *Prologue* provides an anthropology of the soul that combines Dionysius the Areopagite's speculative and anagogic metaphysics with Solomon's practical wisdom of love in the Song of Songs to teach a path of assimilation and union with God. In combining the two, Gallus uses the orders of angels as a means of describing the nature and goals of the human person *and* as a diverse but comprehensive path into God. For Gallus, the soul is, in effect, structured by the angelic orders. In Gallus' spiritual anthropology the angels become gatekeepers through which love comes into being.

The relation of love, or affect, and knowledge is at the heart of Gallus' work with angels in the *Prologue*.[15] All of the angelic orders, from the order of angels to the order of the seraphim, contain and exemplify the various hues and mixtures of heart and mind. All possible permutations of their relation and integration are considered. Thus, for example, Gallus considers the love of knowledge as well as the knowledge of love, making a distinction between what he calls *scire* and *nosse*. *Scire* is love of knowledge, to know, to understand, to be cognizant. *Nosse* is the knowledge of love. It is more practical, experiential, and affective knowledge, but it is knowledge none the less. The highest form of *scire* is found in the cherubim. The highest form of *nosse* is found in the seraphim of the soul, where every other form of knowledge is consummated in the purely immediate kiss which the seraphim, in their burning passion, represent.

But, in structuring the human soul according to the pattern of the angels, Gallus utilizes each angelic order to exemplify something of the relation between intellect and affect. His spiritual anthropology uses, for instance, the category of the 'dominions of the soul' to parallel the activity of the angelic dominions. In Gallus' cosmology the angelic dominions represent the free will and the power to discern good from evil. The powers of the 'dominions of the soul' thus influence both intellect and affect as the soul discerns and makes a decision for good or for evil. The angelic thrones add another dimension to the operations of intellect. Suspended in meditation, the 'thrones of the soul' represent insight beyond reason, described by Gallus as an 'ecstasy of mind' totally receptive to visitations of divine love. For Gallus the 'cherubim of the soul' represent the death of intellect and union with God through 'unknowing'. This, for Gallus, represents fullness of knowledge and the consummation of intellect (intellect is consummated in 'dying' or passing over completely into God), but it does not represent full participation in divine mystery.

Only at the level of the 'seraphim of the soul' is the soul capable of entering into the purity of love and thereby into complete and deiforming union with God. Based on the theoretical vision of Dionysius the Areopagite and on the practical wisdom of Solomon, Gallus equates the seraphic soul with immediate participation and union with God. In *Prologue Y,* Gallus uses the 'burning love' of the seraphim to describe the apex of the affective faculty of the soul and the affective spark within the soul that ignites and brings about the fusion of the soul with God. The seraphim represent a supreme and pure participation in divine Goodness, a flowing of light which descends from God into God's image. The seraphim also represent the contemplative life, an ineffable separation from all that is not divine light, and a passing, so to speak, into the divine life itself. But this is not the end of the journey. The 'end' of the journey brings the soul back to the 'beginning': to the active, ethical life of faith, hope, and charity represented so passionately in the metaphor of the 'kiss'.

However, even in its comprehensive complexity, the celestial hierarchy of angels does not represent the highest route to God. Christ alone is *the* Mediator. Running throughout Gallus' *Prologue,* like a shy shadow, is the assumption that there is no other way to the summit of unitive contemplation than through the *imitatio humanitatis Christi,* that is through affective meditation on the humanity of Christ. Thomas Gallus' project in the *Prologue* is in part to use the angels as a touchstone for a depiction of the human soul quickened and brought to life by the fullest realization of its natural and grace-given powers. But finally, as it is Christ who restores and heals, so it is Christ who most fully mediates human union with God.

Represented by the soul structured according to the pattern of the angels, Gallus teaches that there are many ways and forms of seeing God, each of which is accommodated to our nature. However, there is but one door *into* the Godhead itself: Christ. And according to Gallus, love, as symbolized by the seraphim of the soul, is the key to that door. In the *Prologue* love is the driving force of the soul's journey into God; love is the way, the guide, and the goal. Gallus utilizes the angelic orders, as the various 'lights' from the 'Father of Lights' (James 1:17), to teach the subtle movement of the soul from intellect to knowledge and finally to the full wisdom of the Christian.

CHARITY, QUEEN OF LOVE

In Victorine spirituality compassionate charity is the queen of love. No other form of love is quite like it; no other form is the capstone of theology, exegesis and contemplation in quite the same way as charity. Several medieval Latin words refer to love. *Diligere* means love, yet it has more the sense of 'to esteem' or 'to hold in high regard'. It can also have the simple sense of brotherly love. The word *amor* has, no doubt, the widest family of meanings, but it can best be understood in the sense that it has an object of focus. It can mean love of the world, or love of self, friendship, or even love of God. *Caritas*, or charity, is love which moves outside itself resulting in virtue imbued with knowledge. Charity can be love toward neighbour, love directed toward God, or even God's love for the world. Charity is, therefore, not strictly a kind of love but a way of being, and as such is itself *the* way into God; it is the path of compassion. We have already seen that Richard of St Victor makes love as charity the pivotal force in his mystical and doctrinal treatise, *On the Trinity*. Richard makes inter-trinitarian charity that requires the well-being of another for its very existence the model of perfected love in interpersonal relations.

Love and charity are thus pivotal concepts in many Victorine texts. Two Victorine examples trace the contours of the path of the heart through the wisdom of compassionate charity. The first example is Hugh of St Victor's *In Praise of Charity* (*De laude caritatis*).[16] In this work Hugh begins by admitting that language falls short of the full range of complex meanings of charity. He says at one point that, 'if I undertake to say a few things concerning the glory [of charity] perhaps it would appear that I show more presumption than devotion.'[17] Having admitted his inability to do full justice to the meaning of 'charity', Hugh none the less outlines the following models and paths by which charity may be imagined and imitated:

Introduction in Praise of the Saints:
> Hugh begins by suggesting that the saints (including martyrs and confessors) are models of charity in word and deed. He then shifts the metaphor from imitation to routes or paths into God.

1. Charity is Our Guide to God:
> He admits that from the initial choice to follow God to the final encounter with God is a long and arduous road, but we do have guides. The very practice of charity is our most reliable guide into charity.

2. Charity is the Path:
> Charity is the path of humanity to God, but it is also the path of God to humanity through the incarnation to the passion and resurrection. The power of charity is great because it is the path the love of God chose for our salvation.

3. Charity *is* God:
> Best of all, maintains Hugh, charity is not only the way to God or the way of God, it *is* God. We can say this of no other virtue because charity is the source of all gifts.

4. Conclusion in Praise of Charity:
> Charity descends from God to humanity so that by means of charity men and women may ascend to God. Hugh, admitting the inability of words to fully express the essence or value of charity, ends with a simple prayer of praise.

In a second example, Richard of St Victor in his *Four Degrees of Passionate (Violent) Charity (De quatuor gradibus violentae caritatis)* delves somewhat deeper than Hugh into the nature of charity. Richard claims that not only is God charity, but that in the highest or fourth degree of charity the soul itself is deified and thus is itself made to be 'charity'. If Christ is conspicuously absent in Richard's mystic and contemplative

treatise on the path of the mind, the *Mystical Ark*, here in the
Four Degrees the life of Christ *is* the model of charity.

In addition, unlike Hugh, Richard is not reluctant to make
an attempt to speak comprehensively concerning the nature
of charity. In fact, he is positively giddy about the prospect of
an opportunity to do so. He says:

> I am wounded by love. Love urges me to speak of love.
> Gladly do I give myself up to the service of love and it is
> sweet and altogether lovely to speak about love. This is a
> joyful subject and very fruitful, one that will not weary
> the writer or fatigue the reader. Great is the power of love,
> wonderful the virtue of charity . . . But above all these
> degrees there is that ardent and burning love which pene-
> trates the heart, inflames the affection and transfixes the
> soul itself to the very core, so that she may truly say: "I
> am wounded by love." Let us consider what this surpassing
> quality of Christ's love is.[18]

In general, in Victorine spirituality, charity modelled on the
ministry of Christ is described and discussed in great detail
and precision while the charity that is God is considered
'unspeakable' or ineffable.

Richard calls his first degree of charity 'wounding love'.
Wounding love pierces the affections, restricts thought in that
the mind can no longer resist the desires of the heart, and, as
Richard says, it initiates a 'thirst *for* God'. The second degree
is 'binding love' which causes continual desire for God without
relief. This second degree binds thoughts and weakens activity
but does not eliminate actions altogether. It initiates a 'thirst
to go to God'. The third degree of charity 'excludes every other
kind of love'. This degree of charity destroys actions altogether;
one cannot attend to outward things in that the soul can do
nothing but meditate on love; nothing but love pleases the
soul. The third degree of charity initiates 'the thirst *to be in*
God'. Richard says: 'Therefore the third degree of love is when
the mind is ravished into the abyss of divine light so that the

soul, having forgotten all outward things, is altogether unaware of itself and passes out completely into its God.'[19]

The fourth degree of charity is 'a kind of madness'. Here, nothing at all satisfies the desires of the passionate soul; the soul is, as it were, dead, suffocating from the heat of a burning desire. Even love, as the soul has previously known it, does not satisfy; the desires of this passion are insatiable. This final degree of charity initiates a 'thirst *to be united to* God'. Here in the fourth degree of charity, Richard of St Victor comes as close to deification, as close to complete transformation of the soul into God through Christ, as any Victorine. Using the second chapter of Philippians as his scriptural warrant, Richard uses the images of the kenotic emptying of God taking on the form of a servant in Christ to equate charity with mystical union with Christ through compassion for the world and neighbour. He thus speaks of the summit of divine and human charity accordingly:

> Therefore in the third degree the soul is conformed to the divine light, in the fourth she is conformed to the humility of Christ. And though in the third she is in a way almost in the likeness of God, nevertheless in the fourth she begins to empty herself, taking the form of a servant. In the third degree she is as it were put to death in God, in the fourth she is raised in Christ. The soul in the fourth degree may truly say, "I live yet not I, Christ lives in me" (Gal. 2:20). Such a soul begins to live in the newness of life and "to that person, to live is Christ and to die gain" (Phil. 1:21) . . . Therefore in the fourth degree, the soul is made in some way immortal.[20]

In Victorine spirituality the mind must in some way pass beyond itself to 'touch' God. Through charity the soul walks, as it were, conformed, transformed, and resurrected in the humility of Christ.

The relation of love and knowledge in Christian spirituality has been explored from every perspective imaginable. In the Victorines, we find pathways of the mind *and* of the heart ordered and described in detail unrivalled in psychological and spiritual subtlety. On the one hand, following Augustine, they depict a certain quality at the apex of the mind's powers that does 'touch' God. On the other hand, taking a cue from the negative theology of Dionysius the Areopagite, the highest realities, though most appropriately expressed in terms of the powers of the mind are, for the Victorines, accessible only in a kind of 'ecstasy' beyond or above mind. At other times Victorine writers focus on the route of love. The path of love more often than not is described as the 'highest' route to God; the seraphim as 'love', for instance, always fly higher and in greater proximity to God than the cherubim as 'mind'. This being said, there are two important caveats. First, the paths of love and mind are not really so distinct and separate; they function in tandem, each in turn reinforcing and guiding the other in the soul's journey into God. Second, if the path of love does imply a certain priority, it is a particular form of love: compassionate charity. Such charity integrates action and contemplation, forming a cycle between loving union with God and active service of humankind. In this sense charity toward one's neighbour is not unlike God's love for humanity; it empties itself, taking the form of a servant.

And once again, as we have noted so many times, we cannot really speak of knowledge or charity in Victorine spirituality without speaking as well of these attributes in the context of biblical exegesis, contemplation, the spiritual journey, the apostolic life, the nature of the soul, and theology. It is to the mysteries of theology that we now turn our attention.

5. MYSTICAL THEOLOGY:
THE MYSTERY OF THE REAL

You may hide yourself in a thousand forms,
Still, All-beloved, I recognize you;
You may cover yourself in magic mists,
All-present, I can always tell that it is you.
       Johann Wolfgang von Goethe, 'In a Thousand Forms'

MYSTICAL THEOLOGY

Richard Lischer, in his memoir of early years spent in ministry in a small country church, recounts a particularly memorable funeral service. The service was preceded by accusations and unpleasant arguments between a suspicious congregation, a greedy mortician, the church funeral committee, and himself as a new pastor. The disagreement boiled down to an argument about 'the way they always been done 'round here, forever'. To make matters worse, the burial service itself took place in a pouring rain that turned the cemetery to a lake of mud and the service into a soaked, sombre nightmare. It was a disaster. At the end of the service a mother and daughter climbed the steep side of an adjacent hill in a mist of fog and rain. Together they began to play an old gospel duet on two battered cornets. The notes from the old instruments cut through the mist with surprising effect. Lischer comments:

> When all was lost, Moriah and her mom had recomposed the scene and completed what none of us could resolve. As they disappeared from view, I heard myself whisper, "Thanks be to God." All of Lent lay before us, but now, for

the first time, I could stand in the lumpy mud of our cemetery and see Easter.[1]

There, in the 'lumpy mud of the cemetery', Lischer finds, in the apt words of Nicholas Lash, 'Easter in ordinary'.

Mystical theology emerges from personal experience interpreted in the context of community, the church, Scripture, and tradition. It is not something 'out there', beyond the borders of everyday events; it is an ever-changing answer to fundamental questions – 'who am I and what am I to be?' Mystical theology comes to life in the midst of everyday experience. Such experience may include spiritual practice, reading of Scripture, worship and liturgy, community, and compassion. But it also resides simply in the work-place, in family life, in friendship, through connection with nature, in joy and in sorrow. Mystical theology finds its ground in ordinary things: in dissension within a community, in lumpy cemetery mud, in a simple tune from across the hill.

Today, as we have for centuries, we often 'practise' theology as if it were divorced from our everyday experience. For the most part, theology is even kept separate and safe from 'spirituality'. But it has not always been this way in the Christian tradition.[2] Andrew Louth, writing primarily on the Patristic period of theological formulation, said:

> The formative period for mystical theology was, of course, the formative period for dogmatic theology, and that the same period was determinative for both mystical and dogmatic theology is no accident since these two aspects of theology are fundamentally bound up with one another. The basic doctrines of the Trinity and Incarnation, worked out in these centuries, are *mystical doctrines formulated dogmatically.*

He then remarks, 'it is difficult to see how dogmatic and mystical theology could ever have become separated; and yet there is little doubt that, in the West as least, they have so become and that dogmatic and mystical theology, or theology and "spirituality" have been set apart in mutually exclusive categories.'[3] One of our most astute contemporary writers on the subject of mystical theology defines mysticism in similar terms: 'the mystical element in Christianity [is] that part of its beliefs and practices that concerns the preparation for, the consciousness of, and the reaction to the immediate presence of God.'[4] Other modern theologians, such as Hans Urs von Balthasar, have also given persuasive evidence that the divorce between dogmatic and mystical theology or theology in general and personal experience is, as it was for the church fathers, a false distinction.

Victorine mystical theology provides a model for a mending of the breach between spirituality, experience, and theology. One strategy, taken up in this chapter, for comprehending how this is accomplished in Victorine spiritual or mystical theology, is a careful look at 'positive' and 'negative' ways of speaking about and experiencing God. In line with centuries of earlier mystical theology, Victorine theology uses the language of an approachable, present, and nameable God on the one hand, and an ineffable, mysterious and incomprehensible God on the other hand. It understands symbols as gateways into divine consciousness. It understands contemplation of a diverse and lively creation as a method of experiencing and acknowledging the presence of God. This chapter will focus on the doctrines of creation, Trinity and Christology as the focal points of Victorine mystical theology.

SYMBOLS, DOCTRINE, AND FOOLISH WISDOM

Victorine mystical theology searches for and finds vestiges of the face of God in many places: in creation as sacramental and holy, in biblical revelation, in the image of God in the human person, in the sacraments of the Church, in beauty and in the good, in humility and in open hospitality. Hugh of St Victor's *Commentary on the Celestial Hierarchy of Dionysius the Areopagite*, for instance, is on one level a treatise on symbols and how they serve in contemplation to support the anagogical journey into God.[5] As such, it is an important resource for reflection on the Victorine sacramental world view, on the contemplation of images, and symbolic theology.

Hugh's commentary begins his discussion of symbols by making a distinction between philosophy (what he usually calls 'mundane' or 'worldly philosophy') and Christian theology (what he usually calls 'divine theology'). The distinction is made through Hugh's concentration on Christ as the centre of Christian theology. Hugh remarks:

> And God made the wisdom of this world foolish (cf. 1 Cor. 1:20), since the wisdom of God is not found in this world. God showed another wisdom which seemed to be foolishness, yet it was not. And what was this wisdom? This wisdom was Christ crucified, of whom we preach so that truth might be sought through humility. But the world despised the healer and was thus unable to come to know this truth. Worldly philosophy, certainly, wished to contemplate the wondrous works that God had made, yet was not willing to venerate the works that God had put forth for imitation. Neither did the world attend to Christ's death, but rather sought healing through other forms of pious devotion. It dedicated itself to false healing, presuming to investigate strange, unsuitable things through vain curiosity.

Thus 'mundane philosophy' was able to recognize some aspect of God's reflection, but it continually strayed down false paths. Hugh continues:

> Two Images were proposed to humanity by which it was possible to see invisible things: one is the image of nature and one is the image of grace. The image of nature (available to mundane philosophy) was the outward appearance of the things of the world. The image of grace is the humanity of the Word (available only to divine theology). By both means God is shown, but God is not understood in both ways. Nature demonstrates its art by

means of outward appearances, but it is not able to completely illuminate the eye of contemplation.[6]

Only the 'eye of contemplation' can see the humanity of Christ
for what it is: the grace of God. It is this 'eye of contemplation',
which we first encountered in Chapter Three on exegesis, that
drives Victorine mystical theology. In Victorine spirituality,
theology without contemplative awareness is simply philosophy. Philosophy is important and leads the mind and heart
toward, but not *into* the deep mysteries of God.

By making an additional distinction between the symbols
of nature (available to philosophy) and the symbols of grace
(available only to theology), Hugh is able to link the humility
of Christ to the work of Christ. The work of Christ is, in part,
our access to God, the 'Father of lights' of James 1:17:

> Let us, then, invoke Jesus, the light of the Father, who is
> that truth who "enlightens all humanity coming into the
> world," (John 1:9) through whom we have access to the
> Father, the original light. As much as it is possible, we
> should look back to the enlightenments handed down by
> the Father through the most holy eloquence of scripture.[7]

In Jesus, as light of the Father, all things, visible and invisible,
are manifested to us through the symbols of nature and grace.

This movement from the visible to the invisible world is, as
we have seen, at the very core of Victorine symbolic theology.
Hugh of St Victor defines a symbol as 'a collection of visible
forms for the demonstration of invisible realities'.[8] Richard of
St Victor uses his *Commentary on the Apocalypse of John* to
describe the diverse ways by which one may rise by means of
symbols from sensible things to an understanding of divine
realities. We have already seen some of Richard's work in this
area in the chapter on exegesis: once again exegesis is wed in
Victorine spirituality to theology and contemplation. In the
commentary on John's Apocalypse, Richard describes 'four
kinds of visions' by which the soul may rise to contemplation
of invisible things. In the third vision 'a soul is illuminated by

the Holy Spirit by means of similar forms of visible things through which it is thereby led to an understanding of invisible things.' He describes the fourth vision as that by which 'the human spirit is spiritually led to the contemplation of celestial things.'[9]

These last two kinds of vision are linked by Richard by symbol and anagogy:

> We look upon the manifestation of heavenly souls by means of symbol and anagogy. The symbol is the gathering together of visible forms to demonstrate invisible things. Anagogy is the ascension or elevation of the mind to contemplating the highest things.[10]

We can say that symbols mediate between contemplation and divinity; they are in a sense sacramental conduits leading into the divine presence. Anagogy represents an unmediated and immediate contact or union with God and soul between which there is no intervening form or figure: the union is 'naked' and 'pure'.

There are thus two kinds of symbols in Victorine mystical theology that together illustrate a double aspect of divine mystery. First, there are the symbols of nature illustrating the mystery and grandeur of creation. These symbols show existence of the Creator, but not *what* or *who* the Creator is. Second, there are the symbols of grace illustrating the mystery of the humility of redemption, the 'foolishness' of the cross. The symbols of grace are accessible only through faith. They make known the humanity of the Word, thus showing not only that God *is*, but also that God is *present*. Symbols of grace participate in the restoration of creation by showing the humility of Christ to be the source of all Wisdom and his life to be *the* exemplar of healing, teaching, and restoration.

Both symbols of nature and symbols of grace are given to humanity by God for the demonstration of invisible realities. Hugh of St Victor uses his *Commentary on the Celestial Hierarchy of Saint Dionysius the Areopagite* to prepare the reader for his teaching on symbols as divinely given guides into the light of God. It is difficult to imagine the theology of today insisting that its primary function is the contemplative ascent from the visible things of creation into invisible realities. Yet this is precisely Hugh's teaching.[11] For the Victorines, mystical theology is that 'art' by which we are led from the Easter quality of 'lumpy cemetery mud' to the 'foolish wisdom' of Easter itself.

Hugh of St Victor's *summa*, *On the Sacraments of the Christian Faith*, is at once a doctrinal treatise on the divine works of creation and restoration and an extended commentary on the progression of the soul through history from the Fall to ultimate renewal and union with God. Unlike Athanasius and Anselm who had focused on sin as the primary reason for the incarnation, Hugh focuses on the unity between Christ and humanity:

> On this account then the Son of God was made man, so that between man and God He might be a mediator of reconciliation and of peace. He took on humanity through which He might approach men. The Word indeed, which was one with God the Father through ineffable unity, was made one with the assumed man through a wonderful union. Unity in nature, Unity in person.[12]

For Hugh the unity of Christ with humanity is not only a union of spirit, it is a direct union with the body. The common assumption that early Christianity sought to denigrate or even deny the body in the work of redemption or in contemplative union is simply not true with the Victorines. Hugh is clear that the unity through Christ includes the body. To do this he develops an extended metaphor of unity between spirit and flesh suggesting that the body is the 'mount' or horse upon which the spirit rides into unity with God. In the spiritual journey, the body is the strength of the soul and the soul is the love of the body. Hugh notes that, 'God gave the spirit affection, whereby it might love the body, that, just as it loved the integrity and strength of the body, so also the spirit might freely provide all things which would avail to preserve the body.'[13]

Hugh of St Victor developed and passed on to his fellow Victorines a mystical theology of eschatological restoration and spiritual healing. Hugh describes the journey of healing as it progresses through the evil of sin to gradual correction and consolation. The journey incorporates the 'natural law' manifested in history from the time of Adam to the time of Moses, the 'written law' moving in history from Moses to Christ, and the redemptive time of 'grace' from the incarnation of Christ to the ends of time. His theological depiction of the spiritual journey leads from ignorance to wisdom, from the sacraments of faith to the fruits of charitable virtue. Ultimately, it is a journey of healing as the soul and body are restored in unity to God. Hugh is emphatically clear that the journey is a process of healing: 'Humanity is ill, God is the physician; the minister is the messenger, grace is the antidote, and the vessel of healing is the sacrament. The physician gives, the minister dispenses, the vessel preserves spiritual grace which heals the sick recipient.'[14] In Victorine spirituality, the life of Christ serves as a 'key' or 'window' to healing and divine wisdom. Through Christ all creation and humanity is caught up in the process of restoration, healing, and, finally, union with God.

PARTICIPATION WITH GOD: APOPHATIC AND CATAPHATIC THEOLOGY

Apophatic or negative method and cataphatic or positive method are both at the core of Victorine spirituality, providing two separate but interdependent models of how mystical theology interprets and defines our relation with God and the world. Simply defined, the apophatic way stresses the dissimilarity between God and creature. As a theological position, the apophatic way emphasizes that the all-transcendent God is ineffable, mysterious, incomprehensible, and wholly other. As a mode of speaking about God, the apophatic way denies to God every imperfection found in created things, thus there is no speaking of divinity, no name that fully identifies it, no complete knowledge of it. As a mode of contemplative ascent to God, the apophatic way tells the seeker to 'Leave behind . . . everything perceived and understood, everything perceptible and understandable . . . and strive upward as much as you can toward union with him who is beyond all being and knowledge.'[15]

The cataphatic way stresses the continuity between God and creature and the possibility of divine revelation in the word of Scripture and the Word of Christ. As a theological position, the cataphatic way recognizes that God can be known (if not *what* God is, at least *that* God is) by the light of natural reason, by means of created things, and that God does reveal Godself in accommodation to our nature. As a mode of speaking about God, the cataphatic way states that God must possess every true perfection found in creatures, yet creatures do not possess the perfection of God.

Dionysius the Areopagite[16] is the primary source of both methods in Victorine spirituality. In his principal treatise on cataphatic method, *The Divine Names*, he insists that God does manifest Godself in the world and is 'therefore known in all things'.[17] As a mode of contemplative ascent, cataphatic theology contends that the triune God can be found in all created things as shadows, echoes, pictures, vestiges, representations, or footprints. At the same time the mode of apophatic theology contends that God is above and beyond all ways of knowing and being. Yet it cannot be overemphasized that the apophatic way is inextricably linked to the cataphatic way. The ineffable God *has* spoken a Word; the God beyond words is the same God who 'speaks' creation into being. Thus the transcendent God is also radically immanent; the invisible God was *seen* 'face to face' by Moses and Jacob.[18]

A closer look at how Dionysius links the methods of apophatic and cataphatic theology will help us to understand these ways of thinking about God in Victorine spirituality. Dionysius makes the link very clear: to approach the ineffable

One, one must practise both forms of mystical theology. On
the one hand he emphasizes cataphatic theology:

> In my *Theological Reflections*, I have praised the notions
> which are most appropriate to affirmative theology ... In
> the *Divine Names* I have shown the sense in which God
> is described as good, existent, life, wisdom, power, and
> whatever other things pertain to the conceptual names for
> God. In my *Symbolic Theology*, I have discussed analogies
> of God drawn from what we perceive.[19]

On the other hand, he emphasizes apophatic theology, where
the more one moves toward God, the more language of any
kind falters:

> The fact is that the more we take flight upward, the more
> our words are confined to the ideas we are capable of
> forming; so that now as we plunge into that darkness
> which is beyond intellect, we shall find ourselves not
> simply running short of words but actually speechless
> and unknowing ... the more language climbs, the more
> language falters.[20]

By the end of his *Mystical Theology*, after first considering and
negating the lowest or most obviously false statements about
God, even the most seemingly congruous statements about God
must also be denied. Language, symbols, even Wisdom itself
must be transcended in the ascent from the perceptible to
the inexpressible. Dionysius says, 'It [divine reality] is beyond
assertion and denial. There is no speaking of it, nor name nor
knowledge of it. It is beyond assertion and denial. We make
assertions and denials only of what is next to it.'[21] We cannot
speak fully of God, language falters, we can only say or know
that which is 'next' to God. For Richard of St Victor, this is the
'knowing' which is 'unknowing,' the contemplative practice of
this complimentary method of positive and negative theology
leads finally, as Richard claims, 'into the secret places of divine
incomprehensibility'.[22]

A short meditation can also help us to see interrelation of

divine affirmations and denials. This form of meditation is based on the concept of 'descending affirmations' and 'ascending denials'. That is, in saying what God *is*, it is simpler and more precise to begin by affirming the 'highest' names of God – we can say, for instance, with some ease that God is 'love' and 'truth' – and then *descend* to 'lower' names of God revealed in Scripture but which are, at first glance, not so obviously 'divine' – say, for instance, God as 'wind' or 'rock'. God is referred to as both wind and rock in Scripture, but it is much easier to begin by affirming that God is 'love' and end in affirming that, in a certain sense, God is 'rock'.

Using the *via negativa* or path of denials, the process is just the opposite. In this case, in saying what God *is not*, it is simpler and more precise to begin by denying the 'lowest' names of God – for instance God *is not* 'wind' or 'rock'. These are fairly easy divine attributes to deny: 'wind' and 'rock' seen from this perspective limit who God is and what we can know about God. But we must, to be honest about our limitations and God's transcendence, also *ascend* to 'higher' names of God that become ever more difficult to deny as we go. Thus, after denying that God is 'rock', we must in honesty deny that to our limited way of knowing, God is not really 'truth' or 'love' either. God is *more* than what we can ever know of truth or experience of love. If we started by denying that God is 'love' we would no doubt be uncomfortable with our initial claim. Thus, using love as an example, it is true to affirm that God is love; but it is also true to deny that God is love, because human love, even our most clairvoyant contemplations of love, will fall forever short of God's perfect love and compassion. A chart can help us to see the progression of this meditation.

To practise this meditation, one begins with an imaginative and intuitive meditation on each of the divine names. All human faculties including intellect and affect are brought to bear to 'imagine' the name, to enter into it in all its permutations and contexts, then to either deny or affirm it as a name of God. The meditation continues from name to name as in a

GOD IS:	**GOD IS NOT:**
Descending Affirmations	*Ascending Denials*
Love	Rock
Eternal Wisdom	Dew
Good	Wind
Being	Sun
Truth	Lion
Life	Life
Lion	Truth
Sun	Being
Wind	Good
Dew	Eternal Wisdom
Rock	Love

circle wherein descending affirmations and ascending denials blend one into the other.

How works of Dionysius reached the abbey at St Victor is uncertain.[23] What is certain is that (1) Hugh of St Victor wrote a commentary on Dionysius' *Celestial Hierarchy;* (2) that Richard of St Victor cites Dionysius by name on the *Celestial Hierarchy* in his *Commentary on the Apocalypse of John* (this is noteworthy in that medieval writers in general did not, as a rule, always make a habit of citing their sources); (3) that Achard of St Victor cites Dionysius by name on *The Divine Names* in *Sermon Four*, 'On the Resurrection'; and (4) that Thomas Gallus mentions him often in his *Prologue* to the *Commentary on the Song of Songs* comparing his wisdom favourably with that of Solomon. Beyond these explicit citations it is obvious that, for instance, Richard of St Victor relies heavily on Dionysius in the *Mystical Ark.*

Overall, the Dionysian influence on Victorine spirituality (with some support from Augustine, Boethius, and Eriugena) resulted in a balanced but varied approach to speaking, teaching, and experiencing divine presence. On the one hand the Victorines used images, symbols, physicality, the visible, and the 'thingness' of the created world in their cataphatic or 'positive' approaches to contemplation, theology, and divine union. On the other hand, the Victorines concentrated on the equally important spiritual insight of the invisibility, incomprehensibility, hiddenness and emptiness of God to practise a kind of self-emptying spirituality in their apophatic or 'negative' approaches to mystical theology and contemplation. Though in the medieval period many mystical writers tended to focus on one or the other of these methods of seeking God, the Victorines, especially Richard of St Victor and Thomas Gallus were an exception. Both managed to integrate the two methods. This, of course, leads to a tension both in the spiritual journey and at the very mystery at the heart of God: God is both absent and present, the journey to God takes us into the desert and it leads us to a land flowing with milk and honey. The result of this tension is that, for the Victorines, paradox and mystery are at the heart of human participation with and union in God.

One effect of maintaining the tension and paradox that arise when both the cataphatic and apophatic routes to God are addressed is that God's perceptible glory and God's hiddenness are simultaneous realities. A candle in the dark is just that, a light in the midst of darkness. The darkness defines the light; the light defines the darkness. Richard of St Victor uses the images of night and light to describe the paradox of his contemplative practice: 'This ultimate and highest heaven has its own *day*, however, and certainly it has its own *night* . . . Surely God made the moon and stars in the power of the night, and on that account *this night is my illumination*.'[24]

Apophatic and cataphatic ways of thinking and being do represent a great paradox. But it is a paradox that is at the heart of many religious traditions. The Jewish *Kabbalah*, for instance, states:

> When powerful light is concealed and clothed in a garment, it is revealed. Though concealed, the light is actually revealed, for were it not concealed, it could not be revealed. This is like wishing to gaze at the dazzling sun. Its dazzle conceals it, or you cannot look at its over-

whelming brilliance. Yet when you conceal it – looking at
it through screens – you can see and not be harmed. So it
is with emanation: by concealing and clothing itself, it
reveals itself.[25]

This Victorine form of mystical theology understands that the
'impossible possibility', illustrated also in the Jewish *Kabbalah*
and other religions' mystical writings, is the very ground of
the divine reality. In the *Mystical Ark*, Richard of St Victor
uses the two cherubim atop the ark to represent this paradox.
One cherub symbolizes the divine unity or oneness; the second
symbolizes divine personhood or threeness; one represents
unity, the second represents diversity. Yet *both* are connected
to the ark, *both* are essential to the manifestation of divine
presence that is promised in Exodus. Richard uses the image
of 'hovering' to describe this paradoxical effect of apophatic
and cataphatic method applied to mystical theology and contemplation. Using the example of patterns of birds in flight,
he teaches, as we saw in the previous chapter, that, as with
certain birds, humans can contemplatively 'hover'. In so doing
they become, simultaneously as it were, stillness in motion.
For Richard and the Victorines, it is in this very mode of
contemplative 'hovering' that we are best able to dwell in
wonder and admiration at the various manifestations of God's
incomprehensible wisdom.[26]

MYSTICAL THEOLOGY AS UNION WITH GOD

We have seen that one of the great contributions of Victorine
spirituality is that consciousness of the presence of God is a
way of life. It is nurtured not only in religious doctrine, articles
of faith, Scripture, the living body of the church, and sacraments, but also in knowledge, desire, experience, and virtue.
This insight not only sharpens our vision of the mundane as
potentially sacred; it also points to the possibility of accessing
doctrines as metaphors of mystical consciousness. Religious
doctrine itself is a deep form of spiritual knowledge and experi-

ence. There are no better examples of this than the Victorine appropriation of the doctrines of Trinity and Christology. Both Trinity and Christology function as entry points as well as goals of human perfection and union with God. This Victorine insight has contemplative as well as theological implications, and as we have seen many times, these important implications cannot be separated. We will examine some of the contemplative aspects of Victorine mystical theology in the next chapter. In what follows in this chapter we will observe how these doctrines can serve not only as important theological foci, but also as a kind of 'shorthand' for the awakening of spiritual consciousness in the quest for God and as metaphors of divine union and perfection.

HUGH: CHRIST – THE BOOK WRITTEN WITHIN AND WITHOUT

In *The Sacraments of the Christian Faith,* Hugh of St Victor describes a trajectory of salvation history in which Jesus Christ initiates the 'works of creation' and established and maintains the 'works of restoration'. As he initiates, establishes, and maintains these works, Christ lives perpetually in the will of the Father. His life of obedience takes the form of a servant; in effect his life becomes a model of charity. This model is given to us as an illumination of the possibility of life as constant prayer. Constant prayer represents perpetual consciousness of the presence of God. The ministry of Christ thus demonstrates a kind of theosis or life in unity with God. Of the modelling of Christ for our lives and of the ongoing work of Christ's perfection of the world, Hugh says:

> Christ assumed flesh not losing divinity, and was placed as a book written within and without; in humanity without, within in divinity, so that the book might be read outwardly through imitation, inwardly through contemplation; outwardly according to health and merit, inwardly according to felicity and joy. Within, 'In the beginning was

the Word,' (John 1:1); without, 'the Word was made flesh, and dwelt among us,' (John 1:14). Therefore, there was one book written once inwardly, and twice outwardly. First outwardly through the creation of the world, secondly without through the assumption of flesh in the Incarnation; the first time through creation in order to afford us a pleasurable sight; the second time through the Incarnation to heal us. First in order to create nature, and second, to heal nature that it might be blessed.[27]

According to Hugh of St Victor, Christ is a book written within and without. The 'book of Christ' is 'written' within in the sense of the Word's eternal pre-existence in the inner life of the Trinity. The 'book of Christ' is written 'without' in two ways: creation and incarnation.

The 'book of Christ' can be read through imitation, contemplation, health, or joy. In reading Christ's 'outward books', the 'book of creation' and the 'book of the incarnation', we are given pleasure, joy, and healing. Creation, in this formulation, is good. Thus the incarnation draws creation and humanity into a 'blessed' union; this union is fulfilled in that it includes the Creator as well as the created. This interconnectedness has tremendous implications for contemporary ecological concerns, pointing as it does to our *intimate* relation through Christ with the created world. Meditated upon and followed, the life of Christ, in addition to being the means to full reconciliation with God, is a 'map' that shows us the way to participate with God in all of creation.

RICHARD: THE DOCTRINES OF GOD AND CHRIST AS MYSTICAL AWARENESS

Richard of St Victor's *On the Trinity* is usually considered to be an essential link in the history of the doctrine of the Trinity in the Latin West. Along with Hugh's *Sacraments of the Christian Faith*, it could be considered to be the most purely 'doctrinal' of Victorine writings. Yet, it is much more than that.

It is unique in the Christian West in that it is one of the rare instances of Trinitarian doctrines that start with an analysis of the three persons moving only then toward a discussion of the unity within the Trinity. This direction of analysis is found more often in Greek Trinitarian theology. Richard's *On the Trinity* is often used as an early warrant for contemporary 'social analogy' theories of the Trinity. But more importantly, the real value of Richard's doctrine of the Trinity is its grounding in human interpersonal relations and love. As with all Victorine mystical theology, Richard's Trinity doctrine describes *both* an aspect of divine reality *and* a model of the spiritual journey *as well as* a 'metaphor' of divine participation and union.

Richard's work on the Trinity, with its unique integration of doctrinal and spiritual qualities, deepens our understanding of both personhood and charity. He claims that the very nature of charity indicates that in true divinity a plurality of persons is *necessary*. Richard summarizes:

> Certainly God alone is supremely good. Therefore God alone ought to be loved supremely. A divine person could not show supreme love to a person who lacked divinity. However, fullness of Divinity could not exist without fullness of goodness. But fullness of goodness could not exist without fullness of charity, nor could fullness of charity exist without a plurality of divine persons.[28]

Richard says, in essence, that charity demands a giving and receiving possible only between two or more persons. He uses human love as an analogy of the charity that exists between the divine persons. He is careful, of course, not to equate human and divine love. But in order to justify the necessity of three persons within the unity of the Godhead, Richard draws on the nature of human love in order to describe the perfection of charity and how we might participate in it. Using an image of human love, he notes that the love between lover and beloved is enhanced by the birth of a child. Analogously, the perfection of divine charity between the person of the Father and the person of the Son requires shared delight in the person of the Holy Spirit:

> In order for charity to be true, it demands a plurality of persons; in order for charity to be perfected it requires a trinity of Persons ... Surely it ought to be noted in the divine persons that the perfection of the one demands the addition of another and consequently in a pair of persons the perfection of each requires union with a third.[29]

What sets Richard of St Victor's 'doctrine' of the Trinity apart, lifts it into the realm of contemplative theology, and qualifies it as a metaphor of divine union is his suggestion that the Trinity can be 'grasped' by examining our own experience of shared love. Shared love is itself an experience of self-transcendence; it is an experience of compassionate charity:

> When one person gives love to another and he alone loves only the other, there certainly is love, but it is not shared love. When two love each other mutually and give to each other the affection of supreme longing; when the affection of the first goes out to the second and the affection of the second goes out to the first – in this there certainly is love on both sides, but it is not shared love. Shared love is properly said to exist when a third person is loved by two persons harmoniously and in community, and the affection of the two persons is fused into one affection by the flame of love for the third.[30]

For Richard of St Victor the locus of divine activity is to be found in love and in the community of charity and compassion.

Richard of St Victor's *Mystical Ark* is considered by many to be the high point of Victorine teaching on contemplation and indeed one of the finest works on the contemplative ascent in all of Christian literature. But it is worth noting that in this work as well, the Trinity and the incarnation are used as theological metaphors of mystical union. In fact, as presented by Richard in the *Mystical Ark*, these two doctrines represent the highest forms of mystical consciousness accessible through the grace of Christian contemplation.

In the *Mystical Ark* the two golden cherubim mounted atop the Ark of the Covenant are symbols of Richard's fifth and sixth levels of contemplation. One of the cherubim is a symbol of those things that are, as Richard says, 'above reason'. The second cherub is a symbol of those things that are 'beyond reason'. The cherubim also symbolize the Trinity. One cherubim signifies the 'unity' of God (above reason) while the second is a symbol and route into the mystery of the 'diversity/ personhood' of God (beyond reason): 'It is not by chance that the first cherubim pertains especially to all those things which are considered concerning the unity of supreme and simple divine essence; to the second cherubim however pertain those things which are considered concerning the Trinity of persons.'[31] Again, the two cherubim function for Richard as a symbol of mutual opposition: one cherubim 'gazes' at another because, in the case of the Trinity, unity and personhood, though seemingly opposite, are paradoxically connected. The cherubim are thus a symbol of the very mystery within the Godhead itself:

> Surely in matters of this sort our cherubim turn their faces aside from one or the other aspect, because by a contrary assertion they often maintain diverse conclusions and themselves give assent to opposites . . . According to the first cherub we say that the Father, and the Son, and the Holy Spirit are united in one substance, in one essence, and in one nature. According to the second cherub we say the Father is one person, the Son is another person, and the Holy Spirit is yet another person.[32]

Richard also focuses on the connection between the mystery of the Trinity and the mystery of the incarnation. The doctrines themselves are 'sacramental', holy and sacredly established ways of illustrating divinity as God has chosen to manifest that divinity to us. The Trinity and the incarnation are not themselves symbols. They are mystical doctrines drawn from the tradition and based on experience and critical reflection. Richard uses the cherubim, however, as a symbol of both the Trinity and for Christ since both are grounded in mystery: 'You will find many things like this – and an innumerable amount more concerning the Trinity of persons which are not only incomprehensible but also discordant to reason ... you will also find many things of this kind concerning the union of substances in the incarnation of the Word.'[33] Thus at the highest level of contemplation one encounters not only the Trinitarian mystery but also, represented within the same symbol, the mystery of the incarnation of the Word: one cherub represents the humanity of Christ, the second cherubim represents Christ's divinity.

In Richard's highly developed doctrines of the Trinity and of Christ, the highest levels of mystical consciousness and integration occur. There even seems to be 'slippage' between the two doctrines as the mystic moves ever deeper into the mysteries of the presence of God. The genius of Richard of St Victor in the *Mystical Ark* is to recognize the unity of incarnational and Trinitarian mystery and to integrate the two doctrines through the use of a single symbol: the symbol of the two cherubs. The symbol serves as a kind of 'fulcrum point' upon which Trinity and Christology balance yet 'slip' back, one into the other, on the basis of their shared incomprehensibility. Contemplation on the Trinity acts as a passageway of mystery through which we are led by grace into consciousness of the flesh of the eternal Word.

ACHARD: THE BRIGHTENING OF CHRIST

As a Victorine, Achard of St Victor, like Hugh and Richard, makes no sharp distinction between the figurative use of the imagination, allegory, philosophical theology, and the technical skills of logic developing in the schools of Paris. And also like Hugh and Richard, Achard stretches the meaning and content of Trinity and Christology to include metaphors of mystical consciousness.

We have already seen Achard's elaborate 'building' of the temple within the human soul in Chapter Three. This is also the interior temple that Christ builds within us and which is his abode. For Achard, Christ dwells within us as a threefold participation of the spiritual creature in the Creator. The threefold participation is based on Augustine's Trinitarian exemplarism depicting the divine image within the human soul in terms of power, wisdom, and goodness. Corresponding to these images are Christ's three modes of interior dwelling, also containing Trinitarian overtones: power or love, anointing or spiritual joy, and wisdom or contemplation.[34]

Another metaphor applied to Christ that outlines the spiritual quest for union with God is what Achard calls 'the brightening of Christ'.[35] This lovely metaphor is based on the description of the building of the temple in 1 Kings 5–6. Cedar wood and quarried stone from Lebanon were imported to Jerusalem for construction of the temple. Achard uses the image of Lebanon as a source of 'brightening' or light and illumination (St Jerome gives the allegorical meaning of 'Lebanon' as 'brightening' or 'whiteness'). According to Achard there are two Lebanons: the *material* of wood and stone, which represents the world, and the *form* of wood and stone, which represents Christ. Achard's allegory depicts the journey of the soul from darkness to light under the guiding hand of the 'brightening of Christ':

> Lebanon is interpreted as "brightening". The two Lebanons are two forms of brightening: the brightening of truth and the brightening of vanity; the Lebanon of Christ and the Lebanon of the world . . . The Lebanon of Christ has true brightness; the Lebanon of the world has shaded brightness . . . The brightening of Christ lies in spiritual and true goods; the brightening of the world in carnal and false goods. Hence, the brightening of Christ feasts and enlightens the spiritual eyes; the brightening of the world deceives, destroys and blinds the eyes . . . The first call is from Lebanon to Lebanon; from brightening to bright-

ening; from the illusory to the true; from outside to inside; from the carnal to the spiritual; from the Lebanon of the world to that of Christ. The second call is from a Lebanon beyond Lebanon; that is, from brightening to brightness itself, from the brightening of Christ to the brightness of God. Christ is bright both according to his divinity and according to his humanity . . . There are two darknesses: one of guilt, the other of pain. To these are opposed two brightnesses: one of righteousness, the other of glory.[36]

Achard later notes that Christ dwells within – in our mind, body, and spirit – in many ways. We, in turn, participate in his fullness in many ways: through virtue and discipline, in sweetness and joy, and through the grace of contemplation. Put simply, the indwelling of Christ 'brightens' our path from darkness to light.

As a final example of the Victorine use of doctrine as pattern and metaphor of the spiritual journey, Achard of St Victor devotes a sermon to the soul's passage through seven deserts that bring it to ever-greater intimacy and likeness with God. The passage through the seven deserts restores the divine likeness to every part of our nature, until finally we take on the mind of Christ. The land of promise, reached by crossing the deserts, is in the interior of each human person and those who wander return to this land by returning to themselves: 'This land of promise exists in us; it is the dwelling place of our heart – that is, our inner self – that must dwell with itself in itself – or rather, it must dwell there with Christ who dwells within through faith.'[37]

Crossing the first five deserts represents respectively the renunciation of sin, the world, the flesh, self-will, and reason. The final two deserts represent the contemplative life. In the sixth desert souls find peace, a land of 'milk and honey', discovering themselves in losing themselves, as God is spiritually generated within. These wandering souls die into God so that God comes into them and they into God:

In the present too, from the time people leave themselves

for God's sake, yielding to God and preparing a home for God in themselves completely and not just partially, God follows after them at once and enters secretly. O fortunate exchange! A human being leaves a human being and brings God in. How happy and how gracious a guest! The whole house God enters he fills with happiness and grace ... They leave not from themselves into the world but from themselves into God, so that God comes into them and they come into God. They die to themselves to live to God, and so they live more truly, not in themselves who are shadows, but in God who is truth. They no longer live in themselves, but Christ lives in them.[38]

This is the desert of peace, a self-emptying into which Christ enters, a mystical ecstasy from which one would not naturally wish to retreat. But it is not the final desert. The closer one comes to Christ in love, the more one wishes to imitate his compassion. And so from the peace to the sixth desert, from union with God, one is driven to become perfectly like Christ, a servant to all:

> The seventh spirit, the spirit of wisdom – leads them into this seventh desert that is, of perfect love. In this they are conformed to the wisdom of God, who did the same thing in a much more excellent way, leaving them an example to imitate or to follow. This love is so perfect that none more perfect can be thought of in humanity.[39]

CONCLUSION

In contemplation as in doctrine, Victorine spirituality seeks the mystery 'behind' the real. The 'real' draws the Victorines into the 'lumpy mud' of the world. The power in 'mystery' points ever and always toward a single conclusion: compassion.

Achard of St Victor teaches that to model one's life in conformity with Christ, one moves from love of God to love of neighbour. This movement echoes the central teaching of the Christian faith. As Richard of St Victor also teaches in the

Mystical Ark, at the depths of Christological and Trinitarian awareness one encounters an inalterable commitment to charity and compassion, to social justice, and to the expression of love in the world. The trajectory of Victorine spirituality and mystical theology is not simply from the humanity of Christ to his divinity and through this divinity into the Trinitarian ground of being (though that is certainly an aspect of the journey). The path of the spiritual journey is rather from Christ's humanity to his divinity, into the peace of participation with God, and back to Christ's humanity in an endless generating circle. What the circle generates is compassion and charity, the attributes of divine reality to which all Christian doctrine points.

6. CONTEMPLATION AS A WAY OF LIFE

In his book, *Philosophy as a Way of Life*, Pierre Hadot reminds us that:

> In antiquity, the philosopher regards himself as a philosopher, not because he develops a philosophical discourse, but because he lives philosophically . . . [Philosophy] does not seek to procure a total and exhaustive explanation of all reality, rather it seeks to enable the philosopher to orient himself in the world.[1]

An essential component of Victorine spirituality is to enable the Christian to orient himself or herself in the world in relation to God. For the Victorines, the primary aid to this particular orientation is contemplation. In living contemplatively – as Hadot's philosophers live 'philosophically' – the Victorines orient themselves according to the infinite variety of God's manifestations in the world; they orient themselves on the basis of the contemplative insight that all things are holy. Insight into holiness realigns our priorities toward care for the environment and toward virtue, the sister of understanding. All contemplative insight, whether it be grounded in understanding, virtue, holiness, or love, finds itself most clearly visible in the mirror of charity.

From this perspective, contemplation is the hub of a wheel around which circle various components of the rim that together constitute our lives. The contemplative way of life that sustains a vision of holiness cycles through many stages. Each stage represents, however, not a series of separate concerns but rather different aspects of a single quest to know

God so that we may love God and to love God so that we may serve others.

In this book we have examined the Victorines' vision of the stages of the contemplative life, that circle around the knowing and loving God. We have explored Christocentric and Trinitarian theological doctrines as levels of consciousness that serve as windows to the presence and will of God. Contemplatively considered, these doctrines draw us ever deeper into a kind of partnership with divine knowledge, love, and compassion. The cosmos, Scripture, the human soul, the sacraments and mysteries of the faith – all these serve as symbols of the mystery beneath and within the real. Each, in its own way, aids us along our journey into the sacred: they are 'collections of visible forms to demonstrate invisible realities'.[2]

In Victorine exegesis understandings of history, allegory, the spiritual ascent, and the active life are other examples of the circle of contemplation in the single quest to know and love God. Visual representations of scriptural truths act as images of the soul, maps of the spiritual journey, and contemplative graphics of a revealed route to God. The book of Scripture points to and teaches us to read other books as well: the books of nature, of experience, of the conscience, and of the heart. The spiritual journey and outline of the soul are traced in Scripture, theology, and prayer. 'Charity' becomes 'the full [knowledge] of the law' (Romans 13:10). Love and knowledge intermingle as the 'contemplative' life leads out into the 'active' life and back again. Orders of angels represent levels of consciousness as well as steps in the journey of the soul's awakening.

Contemplation is supported and sustained by all these stages. It grasps as well the paradoxical truth that God illuminates reason yet at the same time is beyond reason; God is light *and* dark, full *and* empty, revealed *and* concealed, present *and* absent, immanent *and* transcendent: God is accessible, perhaps, only through childlike wonder at his incomprehensible mystery. Contemplation as a way of life is simple imitation of the life of Christ that leads to the mystery embedded in the real.

Victorine contemplative practice utilizes the range of human capacity: personal experience, critical reflection, the creative imagination, loving attention, intuitive understanding, and trust in community. Thomas Merton's comment on Scripture – that it is like a vast lake with no bottom – applies to contemplation as well. In contemplating nature, the image of God within, Scripture, or the mysteries of the faith, one encounters deep and loving mysteries within the very 'stuff' of life, mysteries whose depth is never fully sounded.

Given the desperate realities of pain, suffering, and brokenness in this world, love and mystery and wonder may sound slightly naïve as legitimate, let alone attainable goals. Ought we to seek wonder, mystery, or love in the face of such brokenness? Merton's vast lake with no attainable final depth is true in the sense that God, and Scripture as well, know no bounds. But it is also true that the lake has no bottom in the sense that stories of misgivings, false starts, wrong turns, and self-delusions are as much a part of the spiritual journey as are joy and wonder.

In fact, it is the wounds and pain of our lives that shape our personal spiritual journey; the moments of happiness and joy are actually rare. Peter C. Hodgson, in his book on the life and work of the nineteenth-century novelist George Eliot, nicely captures the reality of the manner in which brokenness and pain shape our life. Yet, as he describes them, there are small moments of happiness and joy along the way:

> We human beings for the most part are knotted, mis-shapen, but noble trees. The wounds of life damage and disfigure us but need not destroy us; instead we become stronger at the broken places. We may experience serene happiness and true love, but these are brief moments in the relentless flow of life. We must learn to cherish and remember them, thankful for the gift of life and the all-

provident eye of God that redeems us from our worst moments and saves us for the best.[3]

In charting the course and practice of contemplation, the Victorines were not naïve in claiming the habit of joy and charity. As a single example, we can recall Richard of St Victor's path toward contemplation and compassion as he described it in *The Twelve Patriarchs*. In that work we encountered a depiction of the spiritual journey that wanders and meanders through stages of exile, periods of dryness and desert peril, experiences of fear, grief, abstinence, patience, humility, shame, vanity, bad spiritual advice and discernment, penance, desperate hope, even death. Richard recognizes brokenness and pain; he does not attempt to ignore the reality of suffering. Rather, he incorporates the inevitability of tragedy directly into his itinerary of the spiritual quest. For Richard, as for all the Victorines, contemplation as a way of life travels the paths of brokenness even as it struggles to acquire new eyes through which to view the holy. 'We are all knotted, misshapen trees': this is a Victorine insight as much as it is a twenty-first-century confession. But the *contemplative* element of Victorine spirituality would not, finally, direct our attention only toward our own misshapen growth (though assimilation and acceptance of this quality of the self is essential), but rather to the trees around us, also knotted and noble. It is in this sense that Victorine contemplation as a way of life turns us again and again back to the world, back toward compassion.

As we look at the contemplative spirituality of a few leading Victorines, we will encounter a God whose depth is never completely plumbed, a God who knows us better than we know ourselves, and a God who points us out of ourselves, back toward those twisted, noble, and holy trees around us.

HUGH: VERBAL PRAYER AND CONTEMPLATION

Victorine contemplation initiates a balanced form of prayer. It advocates a middle way between static formalism in prayer and unbridled sentimentality in devotion. Victorines form a synthesis between ordered method and personal freedom of spirit. In Victorine contemplation personal effort is of greater value than simple rote method, yet method serves as a close cousin to effort as it focuses prayer from mere reverie into true mediation. However, it is not personal effort but rather divine grace that 'frees' the spirit for the 'forms' of contemplation. Between method and freedom we find once again that essential element of Victorine contemplation: grace. The subtitle of Richard of St Victor's greatest work on contemplation, the *Mystical Ark*, is *The Grace of Contemplation*. Victorine contemplative teaching always ends with the necessary intervention of grace.

There is a rich interplay between self-understanding, knowledge, love, and wisdom in the Victorine contemplative ascent to God. But we can also look at each as a separate component of the whole. The intellective side of Victorine contemplative teaching is often based on an ordered progression from thinking to meditation to contemplation proper. Forms of Victorine contemplation tending toward the ascent to God through love move more generally from love of the world and self, to love of God, to love of neighbour, and back into ecstatic love of God. The spiritual path leading to wisdom is inevitably tied to both intellect and love, being intimately correlated to ethics and charity.

In all these cases the very possibility of contemplative contact with God is based on the concept of the human person formed in the image of God (*imago Dei*). For the Victorines, this internal image is modelled on the 'perfect image of Christ'. Hugh of St Victor notes in *Noah's Moral Ark* that:

> Christ is life eternal; Christ is wisdom; wisdom is the treasure. This treasure was hidden in the field of the human heart where humanity was made to the image and likeness of the Creator ... Great indeed is human dignity in bearing God's image, always seeing in the self the divine

face and having God ever present through contemplation.[4]

In the *Didascalicon* Hugh combines something of intellect, heart *and* wisdom found in charity when he speaks of five steps whereby the soul moves toward full participation in God: study or instruction (*lectio*), meditation, prayer, performance (works of charity), and contemplation. Study, he says, gives understanding, meditation provides counsel, prayer makes petition, performance goes seeking, contemplation finds. Hugh's own wisdom also shines through in this work as he echoes the advice of so many other Christian saints who teach that the spiritual journey does not always follow a singular path of ascent. He makes it clear that often we must 'descend in order to ascend'. The vicissitudes of life are such that we must often retrace our steps:

> For example: the person who is vigorous in their practice prays lest they grow weak; the one who is constant in her prayers meditates on what should be prayed for, lest she offend in prayer; and the one who sometimes feels less confidence in her own counsel seeks advice in her reading. And thus it turns out that though we always have the will to ascend, nevertheless we are sometimes forced by necessity to descend. That we ascend is our goal; that we descend is for the sake of our goal.[5]

Hugh emphasizes the importance of vocal prayer as an aspect of the process of ascent to God through contemplation. He may think of prayer as somewhat more efficacious than it is described in the following slightly sceptical poem, 'Prayer', by Emily Dickinson, but he would surely have agreed with her that prayer is an instrument that draws us into God's presence and that God is listening and hears our prayers:

> Prayer is the little implement
> Through which men reach
> Where presence is denied them.
> They fling their speech

By means of it in God's ear;
If then He hear,
This sums the apparatus
Comprised in prayer.[6]

In the teaching of novices, Hugh advocates the importance of integrating personal and common or liturgical prayer through a process of acquiring the habit of practising vocal prayer, prayer that 'flings speech into God's ear'. That he should see a relation between contemplation, verbal prayer, and liturgy should not, by now, be surprising. The relation reflects yet another facet of the general integration of all areas of life in Victorine spirituality.

In his short treatise, *On the Power of Prayer*, Hugh speaks of how vocal prayer, or *lectio* on Scripture, can proceed even when the portion of Scripture being prayed seems not to correspond to any particular feeling, question, or issue of the moment. He suggests first that we meditate on human misery and second that we meditate on divine mercy. These two meditations prepare the spirit for prayer, which inspires inner feelings of devotion, regardless of the soul's present circumstance.[7]

Hugh then proceeds to propose nine modes or varieties of verbal prayer grouped in three general classes each distinguished according to whether they make petition in an explicit or in an implied way. The highest class is 'supplication' which is humble and devout prayer in which one speaks intimately with God without petition. The middle class of verbal prayer is 'postulation' which makes a specific petition. The final and lower class of verbal prayer is 'insinuation' which is a simple outpouring of the will through a narration of one's need. The following chart elaborates the various kinds of petitionary prayer in Hugh's treatise:

Nine Varieties of Petitionary Prayer
On the Power of Prayer

Supplication
1. Eager Striving After God
   i.   Complimenting our Need
   ii. In Praise
   iii. Against Adversaries
2. Gentle Entreaty
3. Pure Prayer
   i.   Intense Devotion
   ii. Complete Absorption by Soul's Desire for God
   iii. Forgetting All Needs

Postulation
4. Sincere Entreaty
5. Direct Petition
6. Simple Questions

Insinuation
7. In Fear of God
8. In Trust of God
9. In Contempt of Sin

Liturgical prayer, as noted, is also verbal prayer. For Hugh, it also has this 'prayerful' effect, regulating the words we say in such a way that they correspond to current dispositions and feelings. Beyond that, liturgical prayer is unique as verbal prayer in that it is an activity in which the two principle faculties of the soul, understanding and affect, merge. In liturgy, these two faculties move back and forth alternately, or rather integrate in a kind of complimentary association between the understanding of words and the fever of desire. Elsewhere, Hugh and Richard of St Victor emphasize the contemplative ascent of the intellect to God. In *On the Power of Prayer,* Hugh uses the discussion of liturgical prayer to demonstrate a programme of contemplative ascent by means of the human heart. To climb an 'affective ladder' to God through prayer Hugh suggests a twofold practice: first, verbal prayers centred on personal misfortune through recollection of fear, sorrow, and humility, and second, verbal prayers centred on divine blessing through recollection of joy, wonder, and love.[8]

Knowledge, charity based on the 'knowledge of the heart', and restoration to unity with God are the goals of Hugh of St Victor's programme of prayer: 'The integrity of human nature is attained in two things – in knowledge and in virtue, and in these lies our sole likeness to the supernal [angelic] and divine substances.'[9] The restoration of the divine image and the restitution of human nature are achieved through the work of contemplation as knowledge, virtue, and love which together work to effect the indwelling of God in the human heart, leading in turn to charity. 'Liquefication of the soul' is the felicitous phrase used by Hugh to describe this divine indwelling in the soul reformed by understanding and love:

> The integration of the soul, which has dis-integrated through ignorance, reemerges through thinking, is illumi-nated through meditation, and is finally gathered together again into a whole through contemplation. Contemplation, having liquefied the soul through the fire of divine love, reforms it, pouring out the soul into the mold of divine likeness.[10]

ACHARD: THE WORD IN THE DESERT; BIRTH OF THE WORD IN THE SOUL

Achard of St Victor's 'seven golden columns of inmost contem-plation of the highest good' are outlined in Chapter Three on Victorine exegesis. The context of the 'seven columns of contemplation' is Achard's instruction on the reconstruction of Solomon's temple in the soul of the contemplative. The 'most interior house' of the temple is associated with Christ and is made of the finest gold, described as the 'house of wisdom', representing truth and the divinity of Christ.[11] This inmost house is the 'house of contemplation' supported by its seven columns. In *Sermon 13* where these images occur, Achard says that:

Contemplation of truth is pure gold. Contemplation of truth without any admixture of falsity is gold, pure gold. This kind of contemplation concerning physical creation is pure gold, concerning the spiritual creation is purer gold, concerning the Creator himself is the purest Gold. *Many are the ways of contemplating the Creator,* either by some mode of participation of him, or apart from and above every mode of participation.[12]

One of the goals of Victorine spirituality is to stretch the imagination into perceiving the 'many ways of contemplating' God. With Solomon's temple etched, as it were, upon the heart, the contemplative imagination is able to see the hand of God in all things. We can contemplate, or as Achard says alternatively, 'participate' in God through the soul, through all of creation, through Scripture, liturgical practice, and theology. Alan of Lille, writing very close to the time of Achard, speaks of the multitude of divine theophanies. As with Achard, Alan then breaks into a song of praise that ends 'many are the ways and forms of seeing God'.[13] Both Alan and Achard, in speaking of theophany and contemplation, practically beg us all to *wake up* and see the multitude of paths and ways of seeing God.

We have also seen Achard's sermon on the spiritual journey through the seven deserts. All deserts, in a sense, illustrate a form of discipline and contemplation: they represent 'the many ways', that is, 'of contemplating God'. But it is the final two which taken together represent the highest forms of contemplation. The 'deserts' as an image of emptiness and dryness represent an apophatic path of ascent. Yet at the same time there is positive relational content to the deserts as well. The apophatic and cataphatic modes of contemplation continually revolve one into the other, and there is no better example of this than in Achard's final two deserts. The sixth desert represents an unmediated contemplative union with God that is void of image on the one hand, yet brimming with Trinitarian and Christological content on the other. The seventh desert representing love of neighbour is positively charged by concrete acts of charity yet negatively charged in that the contemplative must in complete humility imitate Christ, who 'emptied himself, taking on the form of a slave' (Philippians 2:7).

Achard also utilizes an extended metaphor of birth to speak of the process of contemplation. This explicit metaphor of the birth of the word in the soul is unusual in Victorine writing, though it is also present in Richard of St Victor in an implicit way.[14] In *Sermon 14* 'On the Feast of All Saints', Achard describes the spiritual journey in terms of a progression from 'feasts of humans', in which the contemplative passes through virtue and action, to the 'feasts of angels' in which reason 'is fully purified'. It is at this point, Achard says, that the soul comes in contact with the purity of the Virgin who is the 'mother of God's contemplation':

> Here, then, the Virgin of virgins comes to meet [the con-
> templative]; she is the immaculacy of immaculacies, the
> purity of purities; that is, immaculacy and purity of heart
> consummated and perfected in accord with what this life
> allows. She is the mother of God; she bears God's Son,
> God's wisdom, God's contemplation.[15]

In the midst of this meeting with the 'mother . . . of God's contemplation', Achard begins to utilize his metaphors of the birth of Christ in the human soul. The metaphors are, of course, based upon and validated by their association with the mother of Christ herself. As is the mother of Christ, so is the purified mind 'virginal'. The mind is thus made 'fruitful' so that when 'aroused' by the Holy Spirit the Son of God may be 'conceived' within the pure mind through contemplation. Achard describes the 'conception' and 'labour' in mystical terms in which the distinction between knowledge and love hardly apply.[16] Using images of both love and mind Achard describes the soul as 'totally inflamed to see the face of God by the ineffable fire of divine love' and later as the mind 'totally rapt, expanded, and raised up' to God. He then returns to the

image of birth as the most apt metaphor for the process of
contemplative union:

> It [the contemplative soul or mind] is in labor as often as
> it has thus conceived a spiritual desire as if placed in the
> light of contemplation; it strives wholeheartedly to burst
> forth into contemplation and, as it were, pass wholly into
> God. It gives birth when it reaches what it strives for,
> when the door is open to the one knocking, when it is
> hidden in the hidden recesses of the divine countenance,
> when, following Paul, it is caught up to the third heaven.
> It is in the first heaven when it conceives, in the second
> when it goes into labor, in the third when it gives birth.
> Or again, after the first heaven of humans, and the second
> of angels, it reaches and enters the third heaven, that of
> the Trinity.

Achard of St Victor thus employs symbolic theology by using
a variety of images to describe the spiritual journey in terms
of contemplation and union with Christ and the Trinity. In
these three short sermons Achard uses three metaphors that
each in their own way describe aspects of mystical union: (1)
building the temple of Solomon; (2) journeys through deserts;
and (3) birth of the Word in the soul. In all three – temple,
deserts, birth – the end result is the same: the ultimate result
of the practice of contemplation is the imitation of Christ's
compassionate charity.

THOMAS GALLUS: THE ANGELIC SOUL AND
CONTEMPLATION OF ANGELS

In Thomas Gallus we find yet another Victorine image used
to structure contemplation: the angelic hierarchy. In Chapter
Two we looked at Gallus' use of the angelic hierarchy as a
'map' of the spiritual journey. In using the angelic hierarchy,
Gallus taps a tradition within Christian spirituality of the
nine angelic orders as descriptions of the spiritual journey into
God. In this tradition the nine angelic orders are not unlike

the ten *sefirot* in the Jewish tradition, or the four-fold path in Buddhism. Each of the nine angelic orders represents not only a particular spiritual path into God, but also diverse theophanic ways of seeing God, ways of ordering the human soul, and nine separate forms or modes of contemplation. Gallus, as with all the Victorines, thus uses symbolic theology to provide an overarching structure of the contemplative method.

The term 'hierarchy' meant a holy principle or ground, but in reference to angels, it meant an organizational pattern in which groups of angels are arranged in a descending or ascending order, for example, seraphim (love), cherubim (knowledge), thrones (discernment), dominions (benevolent rule), powers (courage), authorities (lift up inferior angels), principalities (manifest transcendent principles), archangels (interpret divine enlightenment), and angels (revelation to the world). These nine levels provide the framework of the human spiritual journey. 'Angelic spirituality' consists largely in the awakening of these levels in the human person and in the movement of the soul to greater union with God through contemplation modelled on each angelic order. This is accomplished through the direct ministry of angels and through the correspondences latent in the soul that can be awakened in the spiritual journey.[17]

In the *Prologue* to his *Commentary on the Song of Songs* Gallus provides an anthropology of the soul which combines Dionysius the Areopagite's speculative and anagogic metaphysics with Solomon's practical wisdom of love to teach a path of assimilation and union with God. Gallus uses the orders of angels both as a means of describing the nature and goals of the human person and as diverse but comprehensive contemplative paths. Angels serve both to awaken latent spiritual potential and as 'gatekeepers' through which 'love', 'knowledge', 'discernment' (and so on through the hierarchy) come into being.

Gallus thus uses the angelic orders as levels of mystical consciousness and as objects of contemplation. As mentioned, part of Gallus' intention is to differentiate between the areas of knowledge and love in the contemplative ascent, though the closer we approach to God, the less these categories seem to have meaning or content. Gallus starts with the angels and moves 'upward' toward the seraphim, since it is the seraphim that 'circle in closest proximity' to God.

Gallus sets the stage for the contemplative ascent to God by saying that:

> In order to come to an understanding of Solomon's practical wisdom, it is necessary, by way of a preface, to give an explanation of the following sentence from Dionysius: "I add this, and not unreasonably I believe, that each and every celestial and human spirit possesses its own orders and its own powers according to three levels: primary, middle, and ultimate. By such order and power every human and celestial spirit becomes, by direct participation, the illuminative manifestation of the hierarchies, participating – to the extent that it is possible – in that purification beyond the most sublime purity, in the fullness of superabundant light, and in the perfection which surpasses all perfection."[18]

Gallus' contemplative journey through the angelic hierarchy into God is outlined in Chapter Two. For him, the contemplative, having been 'drawn into the presence of God' through the levels of consciousness represented by the nine orders of angels, participates in that same light that flows through all 'hierarchical souls' awakened to God. As such, the celestial hierarchy serves as a comprehensive mandalic map of the spiritual journey. The Victorine use of symbolic theology, whether the images used are temples, deserts, birth, or angels, clarifies how we experience God. In the hands of the Victorines, these images and the contemplative teachings associated with them, dare us to imagine how we might become more human even as we become more Godlike through them.

RICHARD: INTO THE SECRET PLACE OF DIVINE INCOMPREHENSIBILITY

Richard of St Victor's writing on contemplation would prove to have a more profound influence on future generations of Christian spiritual writers than any other Victorine. Richard deeply affected Thomas Gallus, St Bonaventure, and the fourteenth-century English mystics including the author of *The Cloud of Unknowing*, Richard Rolle, and Walter Hilton. Though his influence cannot be traced directly, it certainly flows through the Flemish and German mystics of the thirteenth to sixteenth centuries and the Spanish Carmelites Teresa of Avila and John of the Cross. Richard's primary definition of contemplation – 'the free, sharp-sighted gaze of the mind suspended in awe and wonder in the visible showings of divine wisdom'[19] – implies that any object is an appropriate focus of contemplation, whether it is of the natural world, of the human soul or psychology, of ideas in the mind of God, or of the Trinity. His teaching on contemplation thus has great potential for contemporary spiritual application.

We have already looked at Richard's teaching on contemplation in the context of the spiritual journey, exegesis, the relation of knowledge and love, and mystical theology. In the *Mystical Ark*, *The Twelve Patriarchs*, and the *Four Degrees of Compassionate Charity,* Richard shows himself to be a teacher and spiritual guide who enters into the world of biblical symbols and mystical theology, making of them vehicles of spiritual instruction and transformation.

Richard's 'Six Kinds of Contemplation' from the *Mystical Ark* are outlined in the chart in Chapter Three. Reference to the chart will be helpful in the discussion of Richard's teaching on contemplation that follows (see p. 000). The *Mystical Ark* is based on Exodus 25 in which God instructs Moses on the construction of the Ark of the Covenant. In this chapter in Exodus, God promises to meet with and speak with his people atop the ark and between the two cherubim. Richard uses this biblical text of divine presence to teach a contemplative method whereby the contemplative may meet personally with and speak with God.

In the *Mystical Ark* Richard uses the Ark of the Covenant and the two cherubim, which sit atop it, as a symbol of the six kinds of contemplation. These six kinds of contemplation are ordered according to the way in which the *object* of contemplation is to be known.

A contemporary Victorine scholar comments:

> For Richard things are known in three ways: through the imagination mediating sense experience; through reason abstracting from sense experience or reflecting on itself; or through the understanding that apprehends invisible spiritual realities that are otherwise inaccessible. Imagination and reason provide knowledge of the visible world and the self. The understanding offers access to a completely different level of experience, the realm of spiritual and divine realities.[20]

The first three kinds of contemplation, symbolized by the wood, gilding, and crown of the ark, represent what might be called contemplation as 'nature mysticism'. In these three kinds of contemplation using imagination and reason, the soul begins to grasp the invisible things of God by means of the anagogic use of visible things of the natural world. In these initial forms, Victorine contemplative spirituality is grounded in the body and the natural world.

Richard then makes a connection between the natural, physical, embodied world and the world of 'invisible things'. These initial stages ground the contemplative life firmly in the physical world. In fact, Richard extends this contemplative 'nature mysticism' to include our own 'book of experience': 'Thus, by means of these things which draw near and give birth to a more evident image of the invisible, we ought certainly to draw a similitude, so that our understanding can ascend through that which we know to that which we do not know through experience.'[21]

There is no doubt that in the last stages of contemplation,

as described and taught by Richard, the contemplative is purged of some aspects of his or her bodily senses. And the encounter with God on the ark between the two cherubim seems at first to take place outside the body. But as we follow Richard, and especially as we keep in mind the incarnate nature of the divinity that is met with and spoken to upon the ark, these lower levels of contemplation begin to reassert themselves. For the Victorines, experience and the natural world are valid instruments by which God's presence can be ascertained. The first three kinds of contemplation thus develop spiritual senses from the initial ground of the body.

The fourth kind of contemplation, also in reason, has for its object the human (and angelic) spirit rather than the natural world. Symbolized by the mercy seat atop the ark, this fourth level of contemplation represents contemplation as 'soul mysticism'. In soul mysticism it is knowledge of the true self (rather than knowledge of nature or experience) that leads to an understanding of heavenly things. As Richard notes, this form of contemplation 'consists in incorporeal things and invisible essences: that is, angelic spirits and human spirits', made accessible to us as creatures because we are 'created according to the image of God'.[22] In this fourth level of mystical consciousness, God is to be found at the core or centre of the self. We have already noted how symbols such as Solomon's temple and the ark represent the process of the inward journey. For Richard one enters into the gate of the self in order to ascend the ladder up to God:

> Therefore, the first thing in this consideration is that you should return to yourself, you should enter your heart . . . This is the gate. This is the ladder. This is the entrance. This is the ascent. By this we enter into the inmost parts, by this we are raised to the heights.[23] . . . And in this way to rise up through a consideration of your spirit to contemplation of spiritual things thus to couple together spiritual with spiritual things, you begin in a similar way to be spiritual.[24]

Functioning in this way, the soul serves as a microcosmic symbol of the macrocosm of heaven and earth. Containing as it does the image of God which serves as a mirror of the divine nature, knowledge of self provides an entry point, a gate as it were, to 'heavenly things'.

The fifth and sixth kinds of contemplation, respectively 'above' and 'beyond' reason, have for their object the humanity and divinity of Christ and the unity and personhood of the Trinitarian God. Transcendence, rather than the natural world or the soul, is the entry point of these forms of contemplation. Symbolized respectively by the cherubim, the fifth and sixth kinds of contemplation represent 'Christ mysticism' and 'God mysticism'. These later two forms of contemplation are wholly dependent on grace.

An important aspect of these last two kinds of contemplation is the angels themselves: they imitate, look upon, model, have first participation in, are granted first enlightenment of, and pass on revelations concerning the divine. But they are not themselves divine. They point toward God, and Richard makes much of the fact that they face each other, looking mutually back upon the mercy seat where God has promised to be present. But they are not God. Richard emphasizes this because, though the two cherubim are attached to the ark and therefore their 'flight' is grounded in the soul and the natural world, in the ecstatic 'showings' of these forms of contemplation the symbol must not be mistaken for the reality. The cherubim *represent* fullness of knowledge, but only God *is* fullness of knowledge.

With this caution in mind, however, the contemplative in a sense 'becomes' these angels, a process of what we might call 'angelization'.[25] Richard uses images such as 'hatching the angelic form' and 'putting on angelic clothing' to describe this process:

> We are able to hatch the form of an angelic likeness within ourselves, suspending our soul in perpetual quickness through wonder at such things and to grow accustomed

to the wings of our contemplation and to sublime angelic flights . . . But in these last two kinds of contemplation everything depends on grace. These kinds of contemplation are distant and exceedingly remote from all human industry, except that each person receives the clothing of angelic likeness from heaven and by divine providence puts them on herself.[26]

Another image Richard uses is that of the contemplative becoming 'a spiritual being of angelic form'. More than the other images he uses this one to indicate the restorative and healing character of transformation. The contemplative begins to become a spiritual being or 'celestial animal' through the angelic clothing of the six wings of contemplation. The first pair of wings cover and protect the body, through them we are still an 'earthly animal'. The second pair of wings, used in flying to the furthest limits of earthly knowledge, indicate that the contemplative has become a 'heavenly animal and has given birth to a heavenly body'. The third pair of wings are given to fly up to the secrets of the third heaven and the hidden things of divinity.[27] With these wings, associated with the six kinds of contemplation, the contemplative, clothed in angelic clothing, becomes a spiritual being with a spiritual body capable of flights 'into the secret places of divine incomprehensibility'.

But here, at the highest level of contemplation, Richard encounters the paradox of divine mystery. On the one hand, only through symbols and images, in this case the cherubim representing 'fullness of knowledge', can we be raised 'above' reason into God. These symbols, in a sense, protect us from the divine brightness: 'I said truly therefore that the cherubim can be said to conceal and protect both sides of our mercy seat, since nothing at all is found in us that is not foreign in quality or incomparable in quantity to the dazzling brilliance of supreme and divine things.'[28] This, of course, echoes the drawbacks of the cataphatic way: images and symbols can lead us only so far. God, finally, is beyond all images and reasoning.

The fifth kind of contemplation, using the symbol of the first cherubim, represents this method of divine contemplation. But, as we have seen, there is also the apophatic way, which is imageless and stresses the unmediated nature of the vision of God. This second way into God is the wordless, direct, apophatic way of contemplation. Here the contemplative, Richard says, is led through ecstasy of mind[29] outside of herself to 'Contemplate the light of the highest Wisdom without any cover or shadow of images, in short, as I have said, not in a mirror and enigma, but in simple truth.'[30] It is in this latter contemplative state of 'ecstasy of mind' that the Trinity and incarnation of the Word are linked, based on their shared mystery and incomprehensibility. Again, at this level, Richard emphasizes the *'grace* of contemplation'. It is through this grace that the contemplative is granted a holy vision or 'showing' of divine participation 'beyond' mind.

Though Richard's contemplative language in the *Mystical Ark* might seem to focus on the mind and mental categories as the primary or only path to God, we know that for the Victorines this is not the only way to 'see' God. Richard uses the language of love and 'bridal mysticism' in the *Mystical Ark*, and his *Four Degrees of Violent Charity* is itself a treatise of the process of transformation through divine compassion and love. Thomas Gallus, to name just one other example, uses the seraphim, which fly in closest proximity to God, as an image of the transformative path of love. Thus it must be said that for the Victorines love and knowledge as distinct and ordered categories simply break down at the highest levels of divine presence. Knowledge, love, images – all these bring us into the presence of God. But language at these heights falters: we can speak not *what God is*, but only of what is *next to God*. The vision of God fuses the categories of love and knowledge even as it transcends them. Objects of contemplation catapult us inward and upward toward God, yet each must be jettisoned as we approach, in the language of the Song of Songs, a final kiss with the beloved. Of contemplation a contemporary writer has said: 'There is an inner dynamic in the evolution of all true love that leads to a level of communication "too deep for words." There the lover becomes inarticulate, falls silent, and the beloved receives the silence as eloquence.'[31]

The graceful and grace-filled Victorine teachings on contemplation all point to the Wisdom of 'silence as eloquence'. All the Victorines, and especially Richard, represent a culmination of centuries of development and also the central paradox of the divine presence: it is a presence that is also an absence, something that can be expressed but is also inexpressible, something, finally, that is most eloquent in its silence.

6. CONCLUSION: IMPLICATIONS FOR CONTEMPORARY SPIRITUALITY

Together, the Victorine masters offer astonishing treasures of spiritual wisdom. Their insights into the spiritual life provide a range of resources for our contemporary quest for meaning, connection, and relationship. A final, brief survey of Victorine teaching can help us begin to assimilate something of the wealth of this spiritual wisdom for our time.

CHARITY AND COMPASSION

In Victorine mystical theology the Holy Spirit is generated in the love between the Father and the Son. Charity, both as it is witnessed and imitated in Jesus Christ and generated by the Holy Spirit, is the hallmark of Victorine spirituality. Charity within and among the persons of the Godhead is understood through human relationship and connection even as it serves as an ideal for human community. As was first indicated in the prologue to this book, the final goal of our spiritual journey is not simply enjoyment of God, but loving service of neighbour. All elements of Victorine spirituality point toward and insist upon 'the greatest of these': love expressed in charity and compassion.

CONTEMPLATION AS A WAY OF LIFE

Contemplation of the divine mystery as it pervades and gives meaning to all aspects of our existence, is a way of life. Contemplation affects the whole life of the individual and of the community, in all the complexities of human relationships. It is not primarily an avenue to perfection, except in the sense that it fosters a desire to realize God's relationship within so that we may witness to God's presence in the world. In this sense contemplation fosters compassion. Contemplation as a way of life integrates the so-called 'contemplative and active' life, recognizing that all of creation is sacred and that the spiritual life – our call to holiness – pervades and gives meaning to all aspects of our life. In Victorine teaching contemplation is deeply relational, positive, inclusive, and recognizes that human and spiritual development are complementary. A delicate balance exists between ordered spiritual practice, the divinely given freedom of the human spirit, and the relational quality of creation, humanity, and God.

MYSTERY AND WONDER

The Victorines cultivated a capacity for mystery and wonder. In fact, their greatest contemplative teacher, Richard, defines contemplation in part as 'suspension in *wonder* over the many manifestations of divine wisdom'. At the ground of each of these divine manifestations, the Victorines find cause to praise and glorify the infinite, divine mystery. Today, in our busy, technological, scientific, narcissistic, and sceptical age, it is difficult, even counter-cultural, to cultivate mystery and wonder. Wonder requires that we admit that something is beyond the ken of our understanding, beyond our personal control. Yet today there is also renewed interest in, and even a craving for, a return of wonder and awe. Ronald Rolheiser, recognizing this contemporary longing, uses the work of the sixteenth-century Spanish mystic St John of the Cross as one way of helping us regain our natural sense of mystery and wonder. He writes:

> The dark night of the soul accomplishes within us a triple task in relation to *restoring our sense of wonder*: 1) It gives

us the asceticism we need to move beyond the dictates of our narcissism; 2) it breaks narcissism and pragmatism as the motivation for our knowing and loving; and 3) it moves us beyond our congenital propensity to relate through conceptual understanding, possessive feelings, and the need for security.[1]

Like St John of the Cross, the Victorines offer us valuable resources for just such a renewed sense of mystery and wonder. The spirituality of the Victorine tradition has a vision of the spiritual journey that awakens us to a world beyond our narrow conceptions of self. It grounds our loving and knowing in the various manifestations of the Wisdom of God. Its assumption of the sacramental quality of the cosmos breaks through the limitations of a perception of the world that sees objects, relations, and values as idols rather than icons. Victorine spirituality combines a gentle claiming of world and self with a renewed sense of the possibility and benefit of letting go of that same world and of the narcissistic self. Victorine spirituality teaches the awe and wonder through the acquisition of new and fresh perceptions. Today we can begin once more to travel along the routes of fresh perceptions into the many ways of seeing God and into the many forms of charity.

THE INTEGRATED SPIRITUAL LIFE

Another exemplary aspect of Victorine spiritual teaching is one we have encountered again and again. This is the integration between secular and religious aspects of life, and, within religion, an insistence on the integration of all ways of teaching, doing, and being. The Victorines utilize secular and 'pagan' truths as a bridge to deeper understandings of theology, exegesis, and culture. Where our contemporary cultures find distinctions between spiritual disciplines, academic endeavours, and practical ways of living, the Victorines find connections. Thus from the Victorines we learn that experience, the spiritual journey, symbolic consciousness, exegesis, love, knowledge, theology, liturgy, the active life or justice, prayer, contemplation, mystical awareness, virtue, teaching, compassion, and the mystery of God's presence are all of a singular, integrated piece and together form a comprehensive 'way of life'.

A SPIRITUALITY OF MUTUAL RESPECT AND GUARDIANSHIP

A variety of Victorine values and practices can be appropriated and utilized in our contemporary culture of 'affluenza'[2] and consequent spiritual hunger. In providing a variety of maps for the spiritual journey, they suggest patterns for spiritual growth that engender respect for others and care for the environment. These maps are symbolic tools for personal growth that awaken and initiate us into ever-deeper levels of mindfulness of the presence of God in all things and in all actions.

Victorine maps of the spiritual journey lead the awakened soul through the created world, into the self, beyond the self into God, and from God back to the world where one encounters both the mystery behind the real and ultimate meaning in community, connection, and relation. As they point to a divine spark in the soul of each person, these Victorine maps of the spiritual journey insist on the sacred value of each and *every* individual. When one asserts the very real presence of the divine image in each and every man, woman, and child of any race, any culture, it becomes deeply contradictory to ignore, pervert or deny the intrinsic value of that individual. Richard of St Victor, for instance, writes of the spiritual journey fol-lowing a path 'into' the centre of the self, there to find the 'presence' of God. His writing is an example of what the Christian mystical tradition has spoken of as journeying 'inward' in order to ascend 'upward' into God. The very assumptions of this tradition *insist* on the sacred humanity of all persons. Richard says:

> Therefore, the first thing in this consideration is that you
> should return to yourself, you should enter your heart . . .
> For at the infusion of this fire [of the Holy Spirit], the
> human soul lays aside little by little all darkness, dullness,
> and severity and it changes over completely into the
> resemblance of that One by which it is inflamed.[3]

Such a journey, drawing us, as it does, to find a 'resemblance
of that One by which it is inflamed' in the face of all those
around us, leads us inextricably into charity and compassion.

These maps of the spiritual journey also formulate a sacramental view of creation that has acute application to
contemporary concerns about the environment and what many
see as an ecological crisis. Obviously, for the Victorines,
creation is good. Without disregarding the fallenness of
creation, Victorine spirituality focuses on the ongoing works
of restoration initiated and maintained in and through Jesus
Christ. Richard of St Victor writes that:

> First the spiritual nature is created so that it might *be*.
> Second it is made just so that it might be *good*. Third it
> is glorified so that it might be *blessed*. And so through
> creation it is started toward the good, through justification
> it is expanded into the good, and through glorification it
> is consummated in the good.[4]

Through the shadow of the vestige of Christ in the created
world, the cosmos becomes a microcosm of the 'cosmic' Christ
who justifies and is restoring creation into the good. The only
valid response there can be to this good is to guard, protect,
and reverence the created world to which we are so deeply
connected.

THROUGH THE VISIBLE TO THE INVISIBLE

Mystery is its own reality. In Victorine spirituality, regardless
of the grace and spirit of our journey, there is always yet
another dimension. There is always *more*. One way to grasp

the Victorine intuition of the 'more' or 'invisible' world and the unfathomable depths of reality in and through the real, is to note the great variety of ways of 'seeing' or 'reading' the world. The Victorines speak of the 'eyes' of the flesh (i.e., our normal way of seeing). But there are other, more acute ways of 'seeing'. We can also see the mystery within the real through the eyes of reason, the eyes of the heart, the eyes of understanding, the eyes of contemplation, or the eyes of faith. The Victorines 'read' the book of experience, the book of nature, the book of Scripture, and the book of Christ. Each of these eyes and each of these books teaches something new, mysterious, and even delightful about themselves, the world, and God. Each of the 'eyes' reading each of the 'books' interprets all of our so-called 'mundane' reality as both what it is in itself *and* as what it points to beyond itself.

GOD: PRESENT AND ABSENT

As thoroughly as the Victorines recognize the sacramental quality of the cosmos – the presence of God in all things and all things in God – so also do they recognize and address divine absence and the very real human sense of loss and abandonment that results. Based on the method of the negative or apophatic path to God, the Victorines address not only the transcendent mystery and incomprehensibility of God, but also this very real sense, in the journey of faith, of the periodic and direct absence of God. Using images such as the desert, emptiness, renunciation, darkness, and what in later centuries would be described as 'unknowing', they combine a humane asceticism with the dialectic of paradox to find processes by which the soul might find and experience 'illumination in the darkness'. Richard of St Victor calls these points of divine illuminations, 'showings'. 'Showings' are nothing more than God's guiding hand. And only at the point where God seems most not to be, can God 'show' Godself to be 'all in all'. In this sense, contemplation as a way of life is a life constantly open, even in the darkness[5] to the possibility of divine 'showings'.

AS ALWAYS, A RETURN TO COMPASSION

As with the majority of Christian spiritual traditions, Victorine spirituality finds its most ecstatic intimacy in Trinitarian and Christocentric reality. Yet these mystical experiences worked out dogmatically always turn us back to the world. They turn us back to a world in need, to a world both real and unseen, to a world dwelling in possibility. Over and over we find Victorine spirituality directing us toward relationship and connectedness. Each path leads to a single possible response: humble compassion. At its most basic, Victorine compassion leads us always forward toward an ever-growing expectation of the holiness of all things.

NOTES

PROLOGUE

1. Bernard McGinn, *The Growth of Mysticism*, Vol. II of *The Presence of God: A History of Western Christian Mysticism* (New York: Crossroads, 1994), p. 398.

INTRODUCTION: A CENTURY OF SPIRITUAL AWAKENING

1. Grover Zinn (ed. and tr.), *Richard of St. Victor: The Twelve Patriarchs, The Mystical Ark, Book Three of the Trinity* (New York: Paulist Press, 1979), p. 2.
2. This book, for the most part, will cite secondary sources and make suggestions for further reading that are available in English. Often the English sources cited will contain more comprehensive bibliographies in other languages. On the twelfth century in general, Gerhart Ladner, *Images and Ideas in the Middle Ages* (Rome: Edizioni Di Storia e Letteratura, 1983), pp. 719–25, contains the most comprehensive bibliographic essay on the issue of the twelfth-century renaissance. Other important and helpful works on the twelfth century include R.W. Southern, *The Making of the Middle Ages* (New Haven: Yale University Press, 1953); Colin Morris, *The Discovery of the Individual: 1050–1200* (London: SPCK, 1972); Tina Stiefel, *The Intellectual Revolution in Twelfth Century Europe* (New York: St Martin's Press, 1985); M.-D. Chenu, *Nature, Man, and Society in the Twelfth Century: Essays on the New Theological Perspectives in the Latin West*, translated by Taylor and Little (Chicago: University of Chicago Press, 1968); G.R. Evans, *Old Arts and New Theology: The Beginnings of Theology as an Academic Discipline* (Oxford: Clarendon Press, 1980); Peter Dronke (ed.), *A History of Twelfth-Century Western Philosophy* (Cambridge: Cambridge University Press, 1992); Urban T. Holmes, *Daily Living in the Twelfth Century* (Madison, WI: University of Wisconsin Press, 1952). Of particular importance for twelfth-century spirituality are Steven Chase, *Angelic Wisdom: The Cherubim and the Grace of Contemplation in Richard of St. Victor* (Notre Dame: University of Notre Dame Press, 1995); Giles Constable, 'Twelfth-

156   *Notes*

Century Spirituality and the Late Middle Ages', *Medieval Renaissance Studies* 5 (1971): 163–74; Caroline Walker Bynum, *Docere Verbo et Exemplo: An Aspect of Twelfth-Century Spirituality* (Missoula: Scholars Press, 1979); Caroline Walker Bynum, *Jesus as Mother: Studies in the Spirituality of the High Middle Ages* (Berkeley: University of California Press, 1982). The comments that follow in the text on the relation of the individual to the group and on the importance of moral example in twelfth-century spiritual formation are based on the work of C.W. Bynum.

3. French scholars undertook much of the original work on the Abbey of St Victor in Paris. *Liber Ordinis Sancti Victoris Parisiensis*, edited by Jocqué and Milis (Turnholt: Brepols, 1984), a compilation for the ordering of the life at St Victor's according to *Augustine's Rule*, provides the earliest source of information on the founding and life at St Victor. The classic study of the founding and history of St Victor, the life and succession of abbots, the life within the cloister, and the school of St Victor is Fourier Bonnard, *Histoire de L'abbaye Royale et de L'ordre Des Chanoines Réguliers de St-Victor de Paris* (Paris, 1907). A good general history of the Augustinian Canons that includes the abbey at St Victor is J.C. Dickinson, *The Origins of the Austin Canons and Their Introduction into England* (London: SPCK, 1950). Most of the English translations of Victorine writings also contain information in outline on the founding of St Victor, the twelfth-century context, and the nature of the Augustinian Canons.

4. On the difference and similarities of Benedictine and Cistercian spirituality see Columba Stewart, *Prayer and Community: The Benedictine Tradition* (London: Darton, Longman & Todd/New York: Orbis Books, 1998) and Esther de Waal, *The Way of Simplicity: The Cistercian Tradition* (London: Darton, Longman & Todd/New York: Orbis Books, 1998), also in this series.

5. Those clergy who did not live a full, common life devoted to poverty and who did not follow the *Rule of St Augustine* were 'secular' canons.

6. The most accessible English translation of the *Rule of St Augustine* can be found in Mary T. Clark (tr. and ed.), *Augustine of Hippo: Selected Writings* (New York: Paulist Press, 1984), pp. 485–93.

7. *On the Formation of Novices* [*De instintione novitiorum*] available in Latin and French translation in Feiss and Sicard *et al.*, *L'oeuvre de Hugues de Saint-Victor* (Brepols: Turnholt, 1997).

8. Clark, *Augustine of Hippo: Selected Writings*, p. 482.

CHAPTER 1. VICTORINE MASTERS: PATTERNS OF INTEGRATION

1. Marcia Tatroe, 'A Crazy Quilt Garden', *Fine Gardening* 8 (April 2002): 54–9.

2. Meaning roughly the 'contemplative life' and the 'practical life'.

3. Recent and well-conceived books on the subject of 'mystical' or 'spiritual' theology include Diogenes Allen, *Spiritual Theology: The Theology of Yesterday for Spiritual Help Today* (Cambridge: Cowley Publications, 1997); Simon Chan, *Spiritual Theology: A Systematic Study of the Christian Life* (Downers Grove, IL: InterVarsity Press, 1998); Mark McIntosh, *Mystical Theology: The Integrity of Spirituality and Theology* (Oxford: Blackwell Publishers, 1998); Philip Sheldrake, *Spirituality and Theology: Christian Living and the Doctrine of God* (Maryknoll, NY: Orbis Books, 1998). This issue will be addressed in greater detail in Chapter Five.

4. Andrew Louth, *The Origins of the Christian Mystical Tradition from Plato to Denys* (Oxford: Clarendon, 1983), p. xi.

5. Allen, *Spiritual Theology*, p. 5.

6. Sheldrake, *Spirituality and Theology*, pp. 3, 15.

7. Cited in and translated in McGinn, *The Growth of Mysticism*, Vol. II of *The Presence of God: A History of Western Christian Mysticism* (New York: Crossroads, 1994), p. 381.

8. Bonaventure, *De redactione artium ad theologiam* 5 (*Opera omnia [Quaracchi: Collegium S. Bonaventurae*, 1882–1902]) 5:3121.

9. On the relation between Richard and Hugh of St Victor see Appendix B, 'Richard and Hugh: Master and Student' in Steven Chase, 'Into the Secret Places of Divine Incomprehensibility: The Symbol of the Cherubim in *De arca mystica* of Richard of St. Victor', Ph.D. Dissertation, Fordham University, 1994.

10. The influence of Dionysius the Areopagite on Richard came primarily through Hugh of St Victor's *Commentary* on Dionysius' *Celestial Hierarchy*. A partial translation of Hugh's *Commentary* is available in Steven Chase, *Angelic Spirituality: Medieval Perspectives on the Ways of Angels* (Mahway, NJ: Paulist Press, 2002).

11. English works that address Richard's life, work, and influence include Grover Zinn (ed. and tr.), *Richard of St. Victor: The Twelve Patriarchs, The Mystical Ark, Book Three of the Trinity* (New York: Paulist Press, 1979); Clare Kirchberger (tr.), *Richard of St. Victor: Selected Writings on Contemplation* (New York: Harper and Brothers, 1957); Steven Chase, *Angelic Wisdom: The Cherubim and the Grace of Contemplation in Richard of St. Victor* (Notre Dame: University of Notre Dame Press, 1995).

12. The Dominican scholar, Gabriel Théry, who died in 1959, has been the person most responsible for the renewed interest in Gallus. Jeanne Barbet, in fact, in her article on Gallus in the *Dictionnaire de spiritualité*, calls Théry the 'inventor' of Thomas Gallus. Cf. *DS* 15, 'Thomas Gallus', p. 800. Théry said of Gallus that he 'transposed into theology that which Dionysius said in philosophy. In a word – and this is our deep conviction – he Christianized Dionysius.'

13. These include: (1) a lost first commentary from 1224; (2) a second commentary written at Vercelli in 1237–8; and (3) a third commentary

written at Ivrea in 1243, the *Prologue* of which is translated in Chase, *Angelic Spirituality*, pp. 241–50.

14. *De septem gradibus contemplationis* written in 1224–6, and the *Spectacula contemplationis* written in 1243.
15. The *Explanations* (*Explanatio*) are currently available only in manuscript form. The *Extract* (*Extractio*) is available in two Latin editions and in Chase, *Angelic Spirituality*, pp. 220–32.
16. Hugh Feiss OSB (ed. and tr.), *Achard of St. Victor: Works* (Kalamazoo, MI: Cistercian Publications, 2001), pp. 23, 30.
17. *Sermon 15,* cited in Bernard McGinn, *The Flowering of Mysticism,* Vol. III of *The Presence of God: A History of Western Christian Mysticism* (New York: Crossroads, 1998), p. 397.
18. Cf. Beryl Smalley, *The Study of the Bible in the Middle Ages* (Notre Dame, IN: University of Notre Dame Press, 1978), pp. 112–20, on Andrew's life and character.
19. From *De Scripturis*, V. 13–5 cited in *ibid.*, pp. 93–4. Emphasis mine.
20. Cited in *ibid.*, pp. 116–7.
21. *ibid.*, p. 125.
22. See Bibliography for examples of translated poems and sequences available in LP and CD format.

CHAPTER 2. MAPPING THE SPIRITUAL JOURNEY

1. *Didascalicon* 3.19, in Jerome Taylor (tr.), *Didascalicon of Hugh of St Victor* (New York: Columbia University Press, 1991), p. 101.
2. *The Celestial Hierarchy, 3.2.* Translated by Colm Luibheid in *Pseudo-Dionysius: The Complete Works* (New York: Paulist Press, 1984), p. 154.
3. Paul Rorem, *Biblical and Liturgical Symbols within the Pseudo-Dionysian Synthesis* (Toronto: Pontifical Institute of Mediaeval Studies, 1984), p. 90.
4. *On the Apocalypse of John [In Apocalypsim Joannis]*, I.1, PL 196.
5. *Commentary on the Celestial Hierarchy of St Denys the Areopagite*, III, PL 175.
6. Cf. *The Extract*, Chapter One in Steven Chase, *Angelic Spirituality: Medieval Perspectives on the Ways of Angels* (Mahway, NJ: Paulist Press, 2002).
7. The outline that follows on the meaning of the various personification allegories in *The Twelve Patriarchs* is drawn from the Introduction in Grover Zinn (ed. and tr.), *Richard of St. Victor: The Twelve Patriarchs, The Mystical Ark, Book Three of the Trinity* (New York: Paulist Press, 1979), pp. 10–22. See also Bernard McGinn, *The Growth of Mysticism*, Vol. II of *The Presence of God: A History of Western Christian Mysticism* (New York: Crossroads, 1994), pp. 401–5.
8. See Zinn, *Richard of St. Victor*, pp. 21–2.
9. A translation of the full text of Gallus' *Prologue* is available in Chase,

Angelic Spirituality which also examines the history, theology, and spirituality in the Christian tradition of the use of the angelic orders as diverse pathways into God.

10. Just a few decades before Gallus, using the cherubim as a symbol of the highest route into God, Richard of St Victor had extended the contemplative aspects of the *imitatio* of Christ to its intellective limits. (Cf. Steven Chase, *Angelic Wisdom: The Cherubim and the Grace of Contemplation in Richard of St. Victor* (Notre Dame: University of Notre Dame Press, 1995), Chapter Five, 'Apophatic Christology'.) And just a few decades after Gallus, Bonaventure would propose that Christ as the supreme Hierarch, incorporating all the angelic theophanies while dwelling in the fullness of his humanity is, through the burning love of his crucifixion, the door, the way, and the goal of the contemplative and active life. (Cf. *The Soul's Journey Into God*, 1.1, 1.6, 4.4, 7.6.)

11. Cited in J. Walsh, *The Pursuit of Wisdom* (Mahwah, NJ: Paulist Press, 1988), pp. 189–90, from Gallus' first *Commentary on the Canticles*.

12. The four stages are introduced in the *Moral Ark of Noah*; the four stages and twelve degrees are presented in the *Mystical Ark of Noah*. In this and what follows I am relying on the work of Grover Zinn in Sommerfeldt *et al.* (eds.), *Studies in Medieval Culture V, 'De Gradibus Ascensionum*: The stages of Contemplative Ascent in Two Treatises on Noah's Ark by Hugh of St Victor' (Kalamazoo: The Medieval Institute, 1975), especially pp. 62–5.

13. Cf. Zinn, *'De Gradibus Ascensionum'*, p. 65.

14. Hugh Feiss OSB (ed. and tr.), *Achard of St. Victor: Works* (Kalamazoo, MI: Cistercian Publications, 2001), p. 50.

15. *Sermon 15.V.19* in *ibid.*, p. 324.

16. Cf. *Sermon 15.VI.34–VII.35* in *ibid.*, pp. 344–8.

17. Feiss, *Achard of St Victor*, p. 55.

18. Cf. *Sermon 15.VII.38* in *ibid.*, p. 350.

19. On the use of the term *manuductio* in Richard of St Victor cf. Chase, *Angelic Wisdom*, pp. 57, 66, 178 n. 38, 196–7 n. 48.

20. Zinn (ed.), *Richard of St. Victor*, p. 53.

21. *ibid.*, p. 124.

CHAPTER 3. EXEGESIS: LITERAL, SPIRITUAL, VISUAL

1. Hugh's *Didascalicon* proposes a rigorous programme of study preliminary to reading Scripture that includes classical pagan as well as Christian authors. This programme was followed by all Victorine masters, each of whom emphasized portions of Hugh's programme depending on their own personality and interests. Briefly, Hugh's programme of study includes all of philosophy which he divided into theoretical, practical, mechanical, and logical knowledge. Theoretical philosophy includes theology proper, mathematics, and physics.

'Mathematics' consists of what at the time was called the *quadrivium* in the schools. This consists of the study of arithmetic, music, geometry, and astronomy. Physics concerns causes and effects in the natural world. Practical philosophy concerns virtue and charity. Mechanical philosophy, or the mechanical arts, consists of fabric making, armament, commerce, agriculture, hunting, medicine, and theatrics. 'Logic' was called the *trivium* in the schools and consists of grammar, dialectic, and rhetoric. Hugh's programme continues by formulating a method of study and suggesting classical pagan and Christian authors who could be read with value. An individual keen on study ought to have natural endowment, willingness to practise, and discipline. Hugh's 'method of expounding texts' might well be considered as a method of study appropriate for today. It includes meditation, memory, discipline, humility, eagerness to inquire, quiet, scrutiny, modesty, and living on 'foreign soil'. With these modest tools in hand, the student was ready to take on the study of sacred Scripture!

2. M. Basil Pennington, *Lectio Divina: Renewing the Ancient Practice of Praying the Scriptures* (New York: The Crossroad Publishing Company, 1998), p. xi.

3. The sequence of the spiritual senses is not consistent in Patristic or medieval exegesis. Often the moral sense is considered to be the height of spiritual awareness, often the anagogical sense is the goal, and at times even the allegorical interpretation is given priority.

4. The first quote is cited in Bernard McGinn, *The Flowering of Mysticism,* Vol. III of *The Presence of God: A History of Western Christian Mysticism* (New York: Crossroads, 1998), p. 375. The second is from Hugh's *In Hierarchiam celestem commentaria* 2, PL 175:941C.

5. Hugh's threefold understanding derives from Gregory the Great through Jerome and Origen. The fourfold tradition derives from Augustine, Bede, Rhabanus Maurus and others.

6. *Didascalicon* 5.2, in Jerome Taylor (tr.), *Didascalicon of Hugh of St Victor* (New York: Columbia University Press, 1991), pp. 110–1.

7. Cf. *Didascalicon* 5.6, p. 127.

8. *The Moral Ark of Noah*, 1.1, cited in Taylor, *Didascalicon of Hugh of St Victor,* p. 223.

9. The comments on Hugh's synthesis and the citation from Chenu are from McGinn, *Flowering of Mysticism*, pp. 375–6.

10. The Commentary, *In Apocalypsim Joannis*, is found in PL 683B-888D. Translations are my own.

11. One such reconstruction of the drawing is available in McGinn, *Flowering of Mysticism,* p. 377. This drawing is based on the important work of Grover Zinn. Other renderings are available in Patrice Sicard, *Diagrammes médiévaux et exégèse visuel. Le 'Libellus de formatione arche' de Hughes de Saint-Victor* (Turnholt: Brepols, 1993). *Libellus* is the *Mystical Ark of Noah*.

12. McGinn, *Flowering of Mysticism*, p. 376.
13. From *Liber exceptionum, Sermon Two*. A larger section of this sermon is available in English in Steven Chase, *Angelic Wisdom: The Cherubim and the Grace of Contemplation in Richard of St. Victor* (Notre Dame: University of Notre Dame Press, 1995), pp. 23–5. Emphasis mine.
14. *Sermon 13.5* in Hugh Feiss OSB (ed. and tr.), *Achard of St. Victor: Works* (Kalamazoo, MI: Cistercian Publications, 2001), pp. 221–3.
15. *Sermon 13.34* in *ibid.*, pp. 251–2.
16. Hugh of St Victor, for instance, speaks at some length on the 'fourfold nature of the soul' (*quaternarium animae*) in his *Didascalicon* 2.4. Other numbers of sacred significance included 1, 3, 6, and 7.
17. *Sermon 13.34* in Feiss, *Achard of St. Victor*, p. 251.
18. *The Moral Ark of Noah*, 1.2. Cited in McGinn, *Flowering of Mysticism*, p. 378.
19. Cf. Grover Zinn, 'Mandala Symbolism and Use in the Mysticism of Hugh of St. Victor', *History of Religions* 12 (1973): 317–41.
20. Cited in Zinn, *De Gradibus Ascensionum*, pp. 64–5, and McGinn, *Flowering of Mysticism*, p. 378.
21. The stages were listed earlier in Chapter Two on the spiritual journey.
22. Table reproduced from Chase, *Angelic Wisdom*, pp. 147–9.

CHAPTER 4. THE PATHS OF KNOWLEDGE AND LOVE

1. Augustine, *Confessions*, IX.10, tr. R.S. Pine-Coffin (New York: Penguin Books, 1961), pp. 197–8.
2. *Amor ipse notitia est*, from *Homilies on the Gospels*, 27.
3. Gervais Dumeige, *Richard de Saint-Victor et l'idée chrétienne de l'amour* (Paris: Presses Universitaires de France, 1952), p. 3. Clare Kirchberger (tr.), *Richard of St. Victor: Selected Writings on Contemplation* (New York: Harper and Brothers, 1957), p. 49, also writes: 'Indeed the twelfth century was particularly interested in the problem of love, love for God and the divine love for man and human love, what the nature of love was and by what word these things may be translated.'
4. *On the Trinity*, 3.3.
5. *On the Trinity*, 3.11.
6. Bernard McGinn, 'The Human Person as Image of God: II. Western Christianity', in Bernard McGinn *et al.* (eds.), *Christian Spirituality: Origins to the Twelfth Century* (New York: Crossroad, 1989), pp. 327–8.
7. This work has been done primarily by French scholars. Cf. Dumeige, *L'idée chrétienne de l'amour* and J. Chatillon, 'Les trois modes de la contemplation', *Bulletin de littérature ecclésiastique* 41 (1940): 3–26.
8. *Richard of St. Victor: The Twelve Patriarchs*, LXXXVI, edited and translated by Grover Zinn (New York: Paulist Press, 1979), p. 145. See

also the chart in Chapter Three on the 'Six Kinds of Contemplation' in Richard of St Victor.

9. On the exegetical tradition of Exodus 25 influencing Richard see Steven Chase, *Angelic Wisdom: The Cherubim and the Grace of Contemplation in Richard of St. Victor* (Notre Dame: University of Notre Dame Press, 1995), Chapter One. On the tradition of the cherubim as a symbol of the highest form or knowledge see Steven Chase, *Angelic Spirituality: Medieval Perspectives on the Ways of Angels* (Mahwah, NJ: Paulist Press, 2002), General Introduction.

10. *The Mystical Ark*, I.xii.

11. These distinctions are not unique to Richard; they are to be found also in Hugh of St Victor and others of the Victorines. Hugh also makes a related threefold distinction: *lectio* (reading), meditation, and contemplation. What is unique to Richard is the degree to which he explored psychological and spiritual elements of contemplation. A chart on Richard's use of the relation of thinking, meditation, and contemplation can be found in Chase, *Angelic Wisdom*, p. 150.

12. *The Mystical Ark*, I.iii.

13. *The Mystical Ark*, I.v.

14. Included among the sources influencing Gallus are the neo-Platonic metaphysics of *eros*, the speculative anagogy of Dionysius the Areopagite, monastic theological preoccupations, the insights into divine theophany and human holiness in John Scotus Eriugena, especially in his *Commentary on the Celestial Hierarchy,* Hugh and Richard of St Victor's work on symbols, aesthetics, and contemplative spirituality, and the Christian strand of affective mysticism exemplified in particular by twelfth-century Cistercian writers.

15. The really extraordinary thing about Gallus in this work is his ability to combine the apophatic, speculative tradition of *intellectus*, the more linguistically cataphatic, imagistic tradition of *affectus*, and the angelic, devotional tradition of *contemplatio*. Cherubic contemplation represents *intellectus* and seraphic contemplation represents *affectus*, but in Gallus the categories interpenetrate: the height of intellective contemplation is regulated by *attracti*, a category of affect, the *apex affectus* is informed by *excessus*, a category of intellect. Gallus says, 'the intellect does not pass beyond touch or a simple surface contact with the divine.' This indicates that the intellect encounters God but is not united with God. The affective portion of the soul, however, is fully united with God. Cf. *Prologue Y, Z.*

16. *In Praise of Charity* is available in Latin with French translation in H.P. Feiss and P. Sicard *et al.* (eds. and trs.), *L'oeuvre de Hugues de Saint-Victor* (Turnholt: Brepols, 1997), pp. 171–207.

17. *ibid.*, p. 178.

18. Kirchberger (tr.), *Richard of Saint-Victor*, p. 213.

19. *ibid.*, p. 228.

20. *ibid.*, pp. 230–1.

CHAPTER 5. MYSTICAL THEOLOGY: THE MYSTERY OF THE REAL

1. Richard Lischer, *Open Secrets: A Spiritual Journey Through a Country Church* (New York: Doubleday, 2001), p. 196.
2. See Chapter One, endnote 2 for a short bibliography of works that both explore the unity of experience and theology in the early Christian tradition and that propose contemporary models for the reintegration of theology and personal experience.
3. Both citations from Andrew Louth, *The Origins of the Christian Mystical Tradition from Plato to Denys* (Oxford: Clarendon, 1983), pp. xiii-xv.
4. Bernard McGinn, *The Growth of Mysticism*, Vol. II of *The Presence of God: A History of Western Christian Mysticism* (New York: Crossroads, 1994), p. xi.
5. The Prologue to Hugh's *Commentary* is available in Steven Chase, *Angelic Spirituality* (Mahwah, NJ: Paulist Press, 2002) pp. 190–6. On symbolic theology in general see Steven Chase, *Angelic Wisdom: The Cherubim and the Grace of Contemplation in Richard of St. Victor* (Notre Dame: University of Notre Dame Press, 1995), Chapter Three.
6. Both passages from *Commentary*, I.1, in Chase, *Angelic Spirituality*.
7. *Commentary,* II, PL 175:933C.
8. *Commentary*, III, PL 175:941B.
9. *On the Apocalypse of John (In Apocalypsim Joannis)*, I.1, PL 196: 686B-687D.
10. *ibid*.
11. Cf. *Commentary*, I.1 in Chase, *Angelic Spirituality*.
12. *The Sacraments of the Christian Faith*, II.I.XIII, in Roy J. Deferrari (tr.), (Cambridge, MS: Mediaeval Academy of America, 1951), p. 249.
13. *ibid.*, I.VII.XIX, p. 130.
14. *ibid.,* I.IX.IV, p. 160.
15. Dionysius the Areopagite, *The Mystical Theology*, 1.1.
16. Dionysius the Areopagite was writing at the end of the fifth or the beginning of the sixth century (though the writings themselves locate the writer in the first century, a companion of Paul). Today, the identity of Dionysius is completely unknown. However, Dionysius' apostolic credentials were unquestioned throughout the medieval period. He was considered to be the Dionysius of Acts 17:34. By the time of the Humanistic movement, the authorship began to be questioned, and it is generally agreed that the denial of Areopagitic authorship by the humanist Lorenzo Valla dealt such a blow to interest in Dionysius that by the time of the Reformation, the reformers had little use for him. He is, however, today enjoying a revival of interest.
17. Cf. VII.3.
18. Cf. Gen. 32:30; Exod. 33:11.

19. *Mystical Theology,* 3.
20. *ibid.*
21. *Mystical Theology,* 5.
22. *The Mystical Ark,* IV.vi.
23. For a survey of scholarship on this subject see Chase, *Angelic Wisdom*, pp. 28–30.
24. *The Mystical Ark,* III.x.
25. Daniel C. Matt, *The Essential Kabbalah: The Heart of Jewish Mysticism*, 'Creation: Concealing and Revealing' (San Francisco, CA: HarperSanFrancisco, 1996), p. 91.
26. Cf. *The Mystical Ark*, I.xii. Richard of St Victor, in fact, uses the two cherubim 'hovering' atop the Ark of the Covenant to signify this incomprehensible Trinitarian wisdom. He says, 'These two cherubim look at each other mutually, because we say that one and the same God is one according to substance and three according to person. According to the first cherub, we say that the Father, and the Son, and the Holy Spirit are united in one substance, in one essence, and in one nature. According to the second cherub, we say the Father is one in person, the Son is another in person, and the Holy Spirit is another in person.' Cf. *The Mystical Ark*, IV.xix.
27. *The Sacraments of the Christian Faith*, I.VI.V, in Deferrari, pp. 97–8.
28. *On the Trinity*, III.II, in Grover Zinn (ed. and tr.), *Richard of St. Victor: The Twelve Patriarchs, The Mystical Ark, Book Three of the Trinity* (New York: Paulist Press, 1979), p. 375.
29. III.XIII; III.V, in *ibid.*, pp. 387–8.
30. III.XIX, in *ibid.,* p. 392.
31. *The Mystical Ark*, IV.xvii, in Chase, *Angelic Wisdom,* pp. 82–3.
32. *The Mystical Ark*, IV.xix, in Zinn, *Richard of St. Victor,* p. 269.
33. *The Mystical Ark*, IV.xviii, in Chase, *Angelic Wisdom*, p. 107.
34. Cf. *Sermon 13.4, Sermon for the Dedication of the Church*, in Hugh Feiss OSB (ed. and tr.), *Achard of St. Victor: Works* (Kalamazoo, MI: Cistercian Publications, 2001), pp. 210–1.
35. The translator of the sermon where this phrase appears notes that the Latin word for 'brightening' and its cognates could also be translated as follows: brightening = illumination; brightness = light; bright = light; brightened = lit. See *ibid.,* p. 222.
36. *Sermon 13.11–13*, in *ibid.*, pp. 221–4.
37. *Sermon 15.6*, in *ibid.*, p. 306.
38. *Sermon 15.34*, in *ibid.,* p. 344.
39. *Sermon 15.34*, in *ibid.*, p. 348.

CHAPTER 6. CONTEMPLATION AS A WAY OF LIFE

1. Pierre Hadot, *Philosophy as a Way of Life: Spiritual Exercises from Socrates to Foucault*, translated by Michael Chase (Oxford: Blackwell, 1995), pp. 22, 27.

2. Hugh of St Victor, *Commentary on the Celestial Hierarchy*, PL 175:941B.

3. Peter C. Hodgson, *The Mystery Beneath the Real: Theology in the Fiction of George Eliot* (Fortress Press, 2001), p. 37.

4. *Noah's Moral Ark*, 3.6. Cited in Bernard McGinn, *The Flowering of Mysticism*, Vol. III of *The Presence of God: A History of Western Christian Mysticism* (New York: Crossroads, 1998), p. 384.

5. Hugh's comments on the steps to contemplation and quote from *Didascalicon* 5.9, in Jerome Taylor (tr.), *Didascalicon of Hugh of St Victor* (New York: Columbia University Press, 1991), pp. 132–3.

6. From *Collected Poems of Emily Dickinson* (New York: Crown Publishers, 1982).

7. *On the Power of Prayer (De virtute orandi)*, 1–5. Available in Latin with French translation in H.B. Feiss and P. Sicard *et al.* (eds. and trs.), *L'oeuvre de Hugues de Saint-Victor* (Turnholt: Brepols, 1997), pp. 126–61.

8. Varieties and affective qualities of petitionary prayer are drawn from *On the Power of Prayer* in *ibid.*, pp. 315, 316.

9. *Didascalicon*, 1.5 in Taylor (tr.), *Didascalicon of Hugh of St Victor*, p. 52.

10. *The Mystical Ark of Noah*, IX, PL 176:697B.

11. Although contemplation is associated with the 'house that Christ builds', Achard is careful to nuance this most interior level of contemplation by saying, 'although the Son is specially described as building the house of God, he does not build it for himself alone, but for the whole Trinity together. Hence he builds not one house, but a triple house.' *Sermon 13.34*.

12. *Sermon 13.32* in Hugh Feiss OSB (ed. and tr.), *Achard of St. Victor: Works* (Kalamazoo, MI: Cistercian Publications, 2001), p. 248. Italics are my own.

13. Cf. Alan of Lille, *Treatise on the Angelic Hierarchy* in Steven Chase, *Angelic Spirituality* (Mahwah, NJ: Paulist Press, 2002), pp. 202–16.

14. Cf. Steven Chase, *Angelic Wisdom: The Cherubim and the Grace of Contemplation in Richard of St. Victor* (Notre Dame: University of Notre Dame Press, 1995), pp. 15–6, 134. Richard's use of the cherubim atop the ark as images of the Virgin's womb has a long exegetical history. Richard, like Achard, also associates the highest level of contemplative birth with the Trinity.

15. *Sermon 14.22* in Feiss, *Achard of St. Victor*, p. 288.

16. This contemplative transcendence of the distinction between knowledge and love is also found in Thomas Gallus in the *Prologue* to the Song of Songs and in Richard of St Victor's *Mystical Ark*.

17. This paragraph is based in part on Ewert Cousins' 'Preface' in Chase, *Angelic Spirituality*, p. 243.

18. *Prologue*, C, in Chase, *Angelic Spirituality*. The citation from Dionysius is from the *Celestial Hierarchy*, 10.3.

19. *The Mystical Ark,* I.iv.
20. Grover Zinn, 'The Regular Canons', in Bernard McGinn *et al.* (eds.), *Christian Spirituality: Origins to the Twelfth Century* (New York: Crossroad, 1989), p. 225. Zinn cautions that 'This use of *understanding* is totally unlike the present-day association of understanding and intellect with reason and rationality. For Richard, as well as Hugh, it is through the understanding that God is inwardly present to the soul.'
21. *The Mystical Ark,* II.xii. The discussion of contemplation which follows can be found in detail in Chase, *Angelic Wisdom,* Chapter Four, 'Contemplation and the Cherubim as Symbol'.
22. *The Mystical Ark,* III.i.
23. *The Mystical Ark,* III.iii.
24. *The Mystical Ark,* III.vii.
25. Cf. Chase, *Angelic Wisdom,* Chapter Six.
26. *The Mystical Ark,* I.xii; IV.ii.
27. *The Mystical Ark,* I.x.
28. *The Mystical Ark,* IV.xi.
29. Richard describes three modes of contemplation 'beyond reason'. These include enlarging the mind, raising up of the mind, and ecstasy or alienation of mind. The first results from human effort, the second from human effort and divine grace, the third from divine grace alone. Ecstasy of mind is caused in three ways: through greatness of devotion, through greatness of admiration, and through greatness of admiration caused by the fullness of spiritual joy. Cf. *The Mystical Ark,* V.ii-xv.
30. *ibid.*
31. Thelma Hall, *Too Deep for Words: Rediscovering Lectio Divina* (New York: Paulist Press, 1988), p. 7.

CONCLUSION: IMPLICATIONS FOR CONTEMPORARY SPIRITUALITY

1. Ronald Rolheiser, *The Shattered Lantern: Rediscovering the Felt Presence of God* (New York: Crossroad Publishing Company, 2001), pp. 99–100. Emphasis is mine.
2. I am indebted to Dr David Meyers for this apt neologism combining 'flue' (sickness) and 'affluence'.
3. *The Mystical Ark,* III.iii, IV.xiii.
4. *The Mystical Ark,* III.xi. Emphasis mine.
5. This said, we need still to recognize that severe depression can crush all hope and openness. Without lessening the overwhelming dread, fear, and anxiety in severe depression, depression is none the less itself a part of the spiritual journey. In the midst of depression, God's grace is neither no more nor no less likely to 'show'.

BIBLIOGRAPHY

Many excellent books and articles in English are now available, though French scholars have done much of the work on Victorine spirituality. Brepols Publishers supports the series, Sous la Règle de Saint Augustin and especially Bibliotheca Victorina, both of which regularly issue monographs, critical editions, and translations on Victorine subjects. Endnote 2 in the Introduction of this volume gives a short but representative bibliography of works on the twelfth-century context of Victorine spirituality.

VICTORINE WORKS IN ENGLISH TRANSLATION

Achard of St Victor. *Achard of Saint Victor: Works*, translated and introduced by Hugh Feiss OSB, Kalamazoo, MI, Cistercian Publications, 2001.

Adam of St Victor. 'Come, Sing Ye Choirs Exultant', in *The Oremus Hymnal*; words by Adam of St Victor, tr. Robert Bridges, music Bourgeois (Genevan Psalm 42), 1950.

—*The Liturgical Poetry of Adam of St. Victor*, translated by D.S. Wrangham, London.

—*In natale* [CD], 'Age of Cathedrals: The Porticos of Light and Worship', *Magnus Liber Organi* Theatre of Voices, directed by Paul Hillier, 1996.

—'Sequence for the Feast of St. Sylvester: Jubilemus Salvatori' [LP], history of European Music – Part I: Music of the Early Middle Ages, vol. 1, *Schola Cantorum Londiniensis*, directed by Denis Stevens, *Orpheus* (Musical Heritage Society), 1969.

Hugh of St Victor. *Commentary on the Celestial Hierarchy of Saint Dionysius the Areopagite, I.1*, translated and introduced by Steven Chase in *Angelic Spirituality*, Classics of Western Spirituality, New York, Paulist Press, 2002.

—*The Didascalicon of Hugh of St. Victor: A Medieval Guide to the Arts*, translated and introduced by Jerome Taylor, New York, Columbia University Press, 1961.

—*The Divine Love (De laude caritatis)*, translated by a religious of CSMV, London, 1956.

—*Hugh of St. Victor on the Sacraments of the Christian Faith (De Sacramentis)*, translated by Roy J. Deferrari, Cambridge, MS, Mediaeval Academy of America, 1951.

—*Hugh of St. Victor: Selected Spiritual Writings*, translated by a religious of CSMV, with introduction by Aelred Squire OP, London, Faber and Faber, 1962.

—*On the Moral Ark of Noah I.2–3* [attributed to Alan of Lille, *On the Six Wings of the Cherubim*], translated and introduced by Steven Chase in *Angelic Spirituality*, Classics of Western Spirituality, New York, Paulist Press, 2002.

—*A Short Preface on the Scriptures and on the Scriptural Writers (Praenotiunculae de scripturis et scriptoribus sacris)*, translated by Denys Turner in *Eros & Allegory: Medieval Exegesis of the Song of Songs*, Cistercian Studies Series, 156, Kalamazoo, MI, Cistercian Publications, 1995.

—*Soliloquy on the Earnest Money of the Soul (Soliloquium de arrha animae)*, translated by Kevin Herbert, Milwaukee, WI, Marquette University Press, 1956.

—*The Soul's Betrothal-Gift (De arrha animae)*, translated by a religious of CSMV, London, 1945.

Richard of St Victor. *Richard of St. Victor: The Twelve Patriarchs, The Mystical Ark, Book Three of the Trinity*, translated and introduced by Grover Zinn, Classics of Western Spirituality, New York, Paulist Press, 1979.

—*Richard of St. Victor: Selected Writings on Contemplation*, translated by Clare Kirchberger, London, Faber and Faber, 1957.

Thomas Gallus. *Extract on the Celestial Hierarchy*, translated by Steven Chase in *Angelic Wisdom*, New York, Paulist Press, 2002.

—*Prologue to the Commentary on the Song of Songs*, translated by Steven Chase in *Angelic Wisdom*, New York, Paulist Press, 2002.

ANTHOLOGIES AND SECONDARY SOURCES CONTAINING SUBSTANTIAL SAMPLES IN ENGLISH OF VICTORINE WORKS

Happold, F.C. (ed.). *Mysticism: A Study and an Anthology*, New York, Penguin Books, 1963. [Richard of St Victor]

Petry, Ray C. (ed.). *Late Medieval Mysticism*, Philadelphia, Westminster Press, 1967. [Hugh of St Victor, Richard of St Victor, Adam of St Victor]

Smalley, Beryl. *The Study of the Bible in the Middle Ages*, Notre Dame, IN, University of Notre Dame Press, 1964. [Andrew of St Victor, Hugh of St Victor, Richard of St Victor]

SELECTED PRIMARY AND SECONDARY SOURCES

Allen Diogenes. *Spiritual Theology: The Theology of Yesterday for Spiritual Help Today,* Cambridge, Cowley Publications, 1997.

Augustine of Hippo. *The Rule of St. Augustine,* translated by Mary T. Clark, *Augustine of Hippo: Selected Writings,* Classics of Western Spirituality, New York, Paulist Press, 1984.

Barbet, Jeanne. 'Thomas Gallus', in *Dictionnaire de spiritualité: ascétique et mystique, doctrine et histoire* 15: 800–16, Paris, Beauchesne, 1991.

Baron, Roger. *Études sur Hugues de Saint-Victor,* Paris, Desclée de Brouwer, 1964.

—(ed.). Hugh of St Victor: *Six opuscules spirituelles,* Paris: Desclée de Brouwer, 1969.

—*Science et sagesse chez Hugues de Saint-Victor,* Paris, P. Lethielleux, 1957.

Berndt, R. *André de Saint-Victor (+1175). Exégète et théologien,* Bibliotheca Victorina 2, Turnholt, Brepols, 1992.

Bok, Nico den. *Communicating the Most High: A Systematic Study of the Person and Trinity in the Theology of Richard of St. Victor,* Turnholt, Brepols, 1996.

Bonnard, Fourier. *Histoire de l'abbaye Royale et de l'ordre des Chanoines Régulieurs de St-Victor de Paris,* Paris, 1907.

Bynum, Caroline Walker. *Docere Verbo et Exemplo: An Aspect of Twelfth-Century Spirituality,* Missoula, Scholars Press, 1979.

—'The Spirituality of the Regular Canons in the Twelfth Century', in *Jesus as Mother: Studies in the Spirituality of the High Middle Ages,* Berkeley: University of California Press, 1982, pp. 22–58.

Cahn, Walter. 'Architecture and Exegesis: Richard of Saint-Victor's Ezekiel Commentary and Illustrations', *Art Bulletin* 76 (1994): 53–68.

Cacciapuoti, P. *'Deus existentia amoris'. Teologia della carità e teologia della Trinità negli scritti di Riccardo di San Vittore,* Bibliotheca Victorina 9, Turnholt, Brepols, 1998.

Callus, Daniel. 'An Unknown Commentary of Thomas Gallus on the Pseudo-Dionysian Letters', *Dominican Studies* 1 (1948): 58–67.

Chan, Simon. *Spiritual Theology: A Systematic Study of the Christian Life,* Downers Grove, IL, InterVarsity Press, 1998.

Charry, Ellen T. *By the Renewing of Your Minds: The Pastoral Function of Christian Doctrine,* New York, Oxford University Press, 1997.

Chase, Steven. *Angelic Wisdom: The Cherubim and the Grace of Contemplation in Richard of St. Victor,* Studies in Spirituality and Theology 2, Notre Dame, IN and London, University of Notre Dame Press, 1995.

—(tr. and ed.). *Angelic Spirituality: Medieval Perspectives on the Ways of Angels,* Classics of Western Spirituality, New York, Paulist Press, 2002.

Châtillon, Jean. 'Les trois modes de la contemplation selon Richard de Saint-Victor', *Bulletin de littérature ecclésiastique* 41 (1940): 3–26.

—*Richard de Saint-Victor: sermons et opuscules spirituels inédits*, vol. 1, Paris, Desclée de Brouwer, 1949.

—'De Guillaume de Champeaux à Thomas Gallus: chronique d'histoire littéraire et doctrinale de l'Ecole de Saint-Victor', *Revue du moyen âge latin* 8 (1952): 139–62, 247–73.

—'La culture de l'école de Saint-Victor au 12e siècle', in *Entretiens sur la renaissance du 12e siècle*, edited by M. de Gandillac and E. Jeaneau, Paris, Mouton, 1968, pp. 147–60.

—*Théologie, spiritualité, et métaphysique dans l'oeuvre oratoire d'Achard de Saint-Victor*, Paris, J. Vrin, 1969.

—'The *De laude libri arbitrii* of Frowin of Engelberg and Achard of St. Victor', *American Benedictine Review* 35 (1984): 314–29.

—*Trois opuscules spirituels de Richard de Saint Victor: textes inédits accompagnés d'études critiques et de notes*, Paris, Etudes Augustiniennes, 1986.

—'Richard de Saint-Victor', in *Dictionnaire de spiritualité: ascétique et mystique, doctrine et histoire* 13: 593–654, Paris, Beauchesne, 1988.

—*Le mouvement canonial au moyen âge. Réforme de l'église, spiritualité et culture*, Bibliotheca Victorina 3, Turnholt, Brepols, 1992.

Chenu, M.-D. *Nature, Man and Society in the Twelfth Century*, translated by Jerome Taylor and L.K. Little, Chicago, University of Chicago Press, 1968.

Denys the Areopagite. *Pseudo-Dionysius: The Complete Works*, translated by Colm Luibheid, Classics of Western Spirituality, New York, Paulist Press, 1987.

Dickinson, J.C. *The Origins of the Austin Canons and Their Introduction into England*, London, SPCK, 1950.

Dumeige, Gervais. *Richard de Saint-Victor et l'idée chrétienne de l'amour*, Paris, Presses Universitaires de France, 1952.

Evans, Gillian R. 'Similitudes and Signification Theory in the Twelfth Century', *Downside Review* 101 (1983): 306–11.

Fassler, Margot Elsbeth. 'Who was Adam of St. Victor: The Evidence of the Sequence Manuscripts', *Journal of the American Musicological Society* 37 (1984): 233–69.

—*Gothic Song: Victorine Sequences and Augustinian Reform in Twelfth Century Paris*, Cambridge University Press, 1993.

Fuehrer, M.L. 'The Principle of Similitude in Hugh of Saint Victor's Theory of Divine Illumination', *American Benedictine Review* 30 (1979): 80–92.

Grabois, A. 'The *Hebraica Veritas* and Jewish-Christian Intellectual Relations in the Twelfth Century', *Speculum* 50 (1975): 613–34.

Hardarson, G. *Littérature et spiritualité en Scandinavie médiévaux. La traduction norroise du "De arrha animae" de Hugues de Saint-Victor*, Bibliotheca Victorina 5, Turnholt, Brepols, 1995.

Healy, Patrick. 'The Mysticism of the School of St. Victor', *Church History* 1 (1932): 211–21.

Hellmann, Wayne. 'The Seraph in the Legends of Thomas of Celano and St. Bonaventure: The Victorine Transition', in *Bonaventuriana I*, edited by Chevero Blanco, Rome, Edizioni Antonianum, 1988.

Illach, Ivan. *In the Vineyard of the Text: A Commentary to Hugh's Didascalicon*, Chicago, University of Chicago Press, 1996.

Javelet, Robert. 'Thomas Gallus et Richard de Saint-Victor, mystiques', *Recherches de théologie ancienne et médiévale* 29/30 (1962/1963): 206–33/88–121.

—'Thomas Gallus ou les Écritures dans une dialectique mystique', in *L'homme devant Dieu: mélanges offerts au Père Henri de Lubac*, Paris, Aubier, 1963, pp. 99–119.

—'Sens et réalité ultime selon Richard de Saint-Victor', *Ultimate Reality and Meaning* 5–6 (1982–83): 221–43.

—'Saint Bonaventure et Richard de Saint-Victor', in *Bonaventuriana I.*, edited by Chavero Blanco, Rome, Edizioni Antonianum, 1988, pp. 63–96.

Jocqué, Lucas *et al.* (eds.). *Liber ordinis Sancti Victoris Parisiensis*, CCCM, 61. Turnholt, Brepols, 1984.

Jollès, B. *Adam de Saint-Victor: Quatorze proses du XIIe siècle à la louange de Marie*, SRSA 1, Turnholt, Brepols, 1994.

Ladner, Gerhart B. 'Medieval and Modern Understanding of Symbolism: A Comparison', *Speculum* 54 (1979): 223–56.

Leclercq, Jean. *The Love of Learning and the Desire for God: A Study of Monastic Culture*, translated by Catharine Mishahi, New York, Fordham University Press, 1961.

Longè, J. *L'abbaye parisienne de Saint-Victor au moyen âge. Communications présentées au XIIIe colloque d'humanisme médiéval de Paris*, Bibliotheca Victorina 1, Turnholt, Brepols, 1992.

Louth, Andrew. *The Origins of the Christian Mystical Tradition*, Oxford, University of Oxford Press, 1981.

McGinn, Bernard. *The Foundations of Mysticism*, Volume I of *The Presence of God: A History of Western Christian Mysticism*, New York, Crossroad, 1991.

—*The Growth of Mysticism*, Volume II of *The Presence of God: A History of Western Christian Mysticism*, New York, Crossroad, 1994.

—*The Flowering of Mysticism*, Vol. III of *The Presence of God: A History of Western Christian Mysticism*, New York: Crossroads, 1998.

—*et al.* (eds.). *Christian Spirituality: Origins to Twelfth Century*, Volume 16 of *World Spirituality: An Encyclopedic History of the Religious Quest*, New York, Crossroad, 1989.

McIntosh, Mark. *Mystical Theology: The Integrity of Spirituality and Theology*, Oxford, Blackwell Publishers, 1998.

Minnis, Alastair. 'Affection and Imagination in "The Cloud of Unknowing" and Hilton's "Scale of Perfection" ', *Traditio* 39 (1983): 323–66.

Moore, Rebecca. *Jews and Christians in the Life and Thought of Hugh of St. Victor*, Atlanta, GA, Scholars Press, 1998.

Newman, J.E. *Achard de Saint-Victor, Sermons inédits*, Paris, J. Vrin, 1970.

Ouy, Gilber, et al. (eds.). *Le catalogue de la bibliothèque de l'abbaye de Saint-Victor de Paris de Claude Grandry 1514*, Paris, CNRS, 1988.

Poirel, D. *Livre de la nature et débat trinitaire au XIIe siècle. Le "de tribus diebus" de Hugues de Saint-Victor*, Bibliotheca Victorina 14, Turnholt, Brepols, 2002.

Ribaillier, Jean (ed.). *Richard of St. Victor, De trinitate: texte critique avec introduction, notes et tables*, Paris, J. Vrin, 1958.

Roques, René. *Structures théologique: de la Gnose à Richard de Saint-Victor. Essais et analyses critiques*, Paris, Presses Universitaires de France, 1962.

Rorem, Paul. *Pseudo-Dionysius: A Commentary on the Texts and an Introduction to Their Influence*, Oxford, Oxford University Press, 1993.

Salet, Gaston, 'Les chemins de Dieu d'après Richard de Saint-Victor', in *L'homme devant Dieu: Mélanges offert au Père Henri de Lubac*, Paris, Aubier, 1963, pp. 73–88.

—(ed. et tr.). [Richard of St Victor]. *La Trinité*, Paris, Editions du Cerf, 1959.

Sheldrake, Philip. *Spirituality and Theology: Christian Living and the Doctrine of God*, Maryknoll, NY, Orbis Books, 1998.

Sicard, P. *Hugues de Saint-Victor et son Ecole*, Turnholt, Brepols, 1991.

—*Diagrammes médiévaux et exégèse visuel. Le 'Libellus de formatione arche' de Hugues de Saint-Victor*, Bibliotheca Victorina 4, Turnholt, Brepols, 1993.

—*et al.* (eds. et trs.). *Hugues de Saint-Victor, Oeuvres, 1: De institutione novitiorum. De virtute orandi. De laude caritatis. De arrha animae*, SRSA 3, Turnholt, Brepols, 1997.

—*et al.* (eds. et trs.). *Hugues de Saint-Victor, Oeuvres 2. Super Canticum Mariae. Pro Assumptione Virginis. De beatae Mariae virginitate. Egredietur virga Maria porta*, SRSA 7, Turnholt, Brepols, 2000.

—(ed.). *Hugo de Sancto Victore, De archa Noe. Libellus de formatione arche*, CCCM-PB 176, Turnholt, Brepols, 2001.

Smalley, Beryl. *The Study of the Bible in the Middle Ages*, Notre Dame: University of Notre Dame Press, 1978.

Taylor, J. *The Origin and Early Life of Hugh of St. Victor*, Notre Dame, IN, University of Notre Dame Press, 1957.

Théry, Gabriel. 'Thomas Gallus. Aperçu biographique', *Archives d'histoire doctrinale et littéraire du moyen âge* 12 (1939): 141–208.

Thoulouse, Jean de. *Le Mémorial' de Jean de Thoulouse, prieur-vicaire de Saint-Victor de Paris*, Bibliotheca Victorina 13–1, Turnholt, Brepols, 2001.

Van Zwieten, J.W.M. 'Jewish Exegesis within Christian Bounds: Richard of St. Victor's De Emmanuelle and Victorine Hermeneutics', *Bijdragen* 48 (1987): 327–35.

Walsh, James. 'The *Expositions* of Thomas Gallus on the Pseudo-Dionysian Letters', *Archives d'histoire doctrinale et litteraire du moyen âge*, 38 (1975): 17–42.

—'Thomas Gallus et l'effort contemplatif', *Revue d'histoire de la spiritualité* 51 (1975): 17–42.

Zinn, Grover A. 'Mandala Symbolism and Use in the Mysticism of Hugh of St. Victor', in *History of Religions* 12 (1972): 317–41.

—'Book and Word: The Victorine Background of Bonaventure's Use of Symbols', in *S. Bonaventura 1274–1974*, Volume 2, Rome, Grottaferrata, 1973, pp. 143–69.

—'*History Fundamentum Est*: The Role of History in the Contemplative Life According to Hugh of St. Victor', in *Contemporary Reflections on the Medieval Christian Tradition. Essays in Honor of Ray C. Petry*, edited by George Shriver, Durham, Duke University Press, 1974, pp. 135–58.

—'*De Gradibus Ascensionum*: The Stages of Contemplative Ascent in Two Treatises on Noah's Ark by Hugh of St. Victor', in *Studies in Medieval Culture V*, edited by Sommerfeldt *et al.*, Kalamazoo, The Medieval Institute, 1975, pp. 61–79.

—'Personification Allegory and Visions of Light in Richard of St. Victor's Teaching on Contemplation', *University of Toronto Quarterly* 46 (1977): 190–214.

—'History and Interpretation: "Hebrew Truth", Judaism, and the Victorine Exegetical Tradition', in *Jews and Christians: Exploring the Past, Present, and Future,* edited by J.H. Charlesworth, New York, Crossroad, 1990, pp. 100–23.

—'Hugh of St. Victor, Isaiah's Vision, and *De arca Noe*', in *The Church and the Arts*, edited by Diana Wood, New York, Blackwell Publishers, 1992.

—'Exegesis and Spirituality in Richard of St. Victor', in *Doors of Understanding; Conversations in Global Spirituality in Honor of Ewert Cousins*, edited by Steven Chase, Quincy IL, Franciscan Press, 1997, pp. 127–44.